More Praise for

"*The Soul Solution* is a beautiful, heartfelt, clear, wonderful guide to resolving our problems and challenges in life. Jonathan Parker shows us that the solution is simple, something everyone can do. I highly recommend this book to everyone on the entire planet."

— Marc Allen, author of *The Greatest Secret of All*

"This wonderfully inspired yet eminently practical guide will take you on a journey directly to the Soul."

— Diana Lang, author of *Opening to Meditation*

To
Rick – my
inspiration!

Love Susan x

the

SOUL
SOLUTION

the SOUL SOLUTION

ENLIGHTENING MEDITATIONS
FOR RESOLVING LIFE'S PROBLEMS

JONATHAN PARKER

H J Kramer

published in a joint venture with

New World Library
Novato, California

H J Kramer

published in a joint venture with

New World Library

Editorial office: Administrative office:
H J Kramer   New World Library
P.O. Box 1082'   14 Pamaron Way
Tiburon, California 94920   Novato, California 94949

Edited by Nancy Carleton and Jeff Campbell
Text design by Tona Pearce Myers

Library of Congress in Cataloging Publication Data
Parker, Jonathan.
  The soul solution : enlightening meditations for resolving life's problems / Jonathan Parker.
    p.   cm.
  ISBN 978-1-932073-52-2 (pbk. : alk. paper)
  1. Meditations. 2. Soul. I. Title.
  BL624.2.P37 2011
  158.1'2—dc23   2011017935

First printing, August 2011
ISBN 978-1-932073-52-2
Printed in Canada on 100% postconsumer-waste recycled paper

10 9 8 7 6 5 4 3 2 1

This book is dedicated to you
whose soul yearns to awaken

CONTENTS

PART THREE
THE SOUL-SOLUTION GUIDE TO HEALING
AND ENLIGHTENMENT

ACKNOWLEDGMENTS

There are many who have contributed to this book's creation, but I first of all want to acknowledge and thank the many who have attended my workshops, classes, and retreats, as well as those who have spent many hours with me in soul-searching meditations and private sessions.

I most especially want to express my deepest love and gratitude for my greatest teacher, friend, and beloved wife, Jackie, for her generous spirit, loving support, and meaningful suggestions, which enabled me to refine this book and delve into the depths of the soul and spirit.

In addition, my lifelong friend and literary professor David Joplin's suggestions and comments were invaluable in the preparation of the manuscript. His recommendations were a great help, and his friendship and support have been most important to me.

Most certainly of no less importance is Nancy Carleton, whose depth of insight and experience were a most valued contribution to refining *The Soul Solution*. She greatly helped me translate many of the concepts I have used in my workshops and private sessions into easily accessible written language.

I am also grateful for my assistant Karen Shulman for her always cheerful spirit and helpful voice in answering countless questions and phone calls for me for more than twenty years.

I send my deep appreciation to Renee Swisko, a remarkable healer and friend, who encouraged me from the earliest stages of this book with many supportive recommendations.

The publication of a book can only happen with a wonderful team, and Georgia Hughes, Tracy Cunningham, Kristen Cashman, Jonathan Wichmann, Tona Pearce Myers, Kim Corbin, freelance editor Jeff Campbell, and others at New World Library have been most supportive in bringing *The Soul Solution* to the world.

And my deep gratitude goes to the vision and suggestions of Linda Kramer, whose guiding light is responsible for bringing this book to publication.

PREFACE

W ho are you? Where did you come from? Why are you here, and where are you going? Are you just a body with a compilation of memories? Each time you explore these questions, you enter the deepest mysteries of human existence and realize that there's much more to you than can be explained through the workings of body and mind.

I'm an author, counselor, and spiritual teacher who has spent the past several decades exploring these deep questions. I've been on many remarkable journeys, which have included spontaneous shifts in consciousness, to discover the miraculous transformational and healing qualities of the soul, which I share with you in *The Soul Solution*. As you follow the processes in this book, you'll experience your own realizations, bringing a deep and rich awakening to all your soul has to offer.

You are more than your body and your mind. Who you are is found in the core of your soul. Your soul already contains the many wonderful and beautiful qualities that we admire in saints, spiritual leaders, and revered teachers, and as you deepen your relationship with your soul through the soul-solution process, these qualities will automatically — and quite naturally — emerge in your life as a result.

For more than thirty years, I've refined the soul-solution techniques through classes, workshops, and thousands of counseling sessions to reveal the secrets to clearing the control and dominance of the ego. By tapping into simple meditative techniques and attuning to your soul, you can merge with the soul's presence and spontaneously release painful thoughts, memories, and emotions and live fully in the present moment. Using the meditations in this book, not only can you explore and heal painful childhood patterns, but you can soar to the heights of enlightenment through spiritual surrender. I'll show you how to access the power of grace to discover all of the soul's gifts.

A VISION OF LIGHT

So that you can better understand why I believe that knowledge of and connection with the soul are so important, let me share with you how I came to have a deeper understanding of it. In the fall of 2002, I was leading a two-week meditation retreat at Mt. Shasta, which is in Northern California a bit south of the Oregon border. Mt. Shasta has a reputation as one of the world's sacred mountains. Many books describe the spiritual experiences that people have had on this mountain, and I was aware of the mountain's power and had already conducted dozens of retreats, workshops, and classes there.

At that point in my life, I'd been on a dedicated spiritual path for some forty years, and I'd been working for many years as a counselor and teacher, and yet my experience that fall of 2002 opened me up to a new level of what's possible. I had arrived at this retreat with the specific intention of finding a way to help more people with their physical and emotional problems. Beyond that, I held the intention of wanting to be shown how I could facilitate miracles to help people, and specifically how I could connect with the same miraculous Source that biblical personalities had used two thousand or more years ago.

One particular evening while I was meditating, I had an incredible vision in which I saw the entire universe opening up before me. A brilliant light blazed into and all around me. The light filled me from head to toe, putting me into a remarkably euphoric state. I saw thousands of angels and what appeared to be a huge opening, much like a rip in the fabric of the universe. In that moment, I knew that this was an opening to the divine Source, which would enable direct access to the light and power of God, and which I have come to understand as the *light of the soul*.

This experience burned an impression into my mind so clear and powerful that even years later I'm still fully aware of it, and I can still see it in my mind's eye as if it has just happened.

I know this may sound remarkable, perhaps even unbelievable. Some might think that perhaps I simply experienced a hallucination, but I was wide awake and my mind clear at the time. I was perhaps more aware, awake, and clear minded than I'd ever been before.

Throughout the centuries, spiritual truths and teachings of all traditions have become lost in ritual and ceremony to a point where much of religion has been reduced to books of rules and outward forms, stripped of the power to reconnect people to their divine nature, so it's natural that people are sometimes skeptical about spiritual experiences. The word *religion* itself comes from the Latin root *religare*, which means to tie, fasten, or bind, and it refers to reconnecting with our divinity. Yet to a great degree, most religions have lost this underpinning. What I learned on Mt. Shasta is that the power of our divine nature is available to anyone who desires to access it.

I certainly don't consider myself to be special in any way, nor do I claim to be the only one who has made the discovery of the subtle energetic presence that's the subject of this book. I'm simply relating what happened to me while I was meditating and praying in all sincerity to be shown a better way of helping people, and I can definitely say that a way was shown to me, and in quite a dramatic fashion!

The day after I experienced this vision, I was doing a counseling session with a woman at the retreat. She commented to me that my energy felt stronger in some way. She was experiencing great emotional turmoil in her life, and I was in the process of helping her through it in our session, when she felt a spontaneous release and lightness.

At the time, I didn't fully understand what had happened to me during the vision, but my experience with this woman made me realize that something significant had taken place. I was able to share the experience of the energy I'd encountered with others.

Over the next several weeks, I did many counseling sessions, and my clients reported similar experiences. It became more and more obvious that what had happened to me as a result of my vision on Mt. Shasta was having a significant impact on others. Over the following months, I realized that my telling people the story of my vision and asking them to be open to receiving the light of their soul led them to have profound, transformative experiences of their own.

This book is the natural progression of my work to help others improve their lives. In it, I describe the meditation practices

I've developed in the years following that Mt. Shasta retreat. *The Soul Solution* provides easy, how-to guidance to help you become an empowered person as you melt the core of ego defenses and life blockages that keep you from achieving peace, happiness, success, and self-realization. Step-by-step, you'll replace these defenses and blockages with practical and enlightened soul qualities.

The Soul Solution reveals deep spiritual wisdom, resources, and self-guided practices to transform consciousness and enlighten you in order to create deep love, fulfillment, and harmony. It's time to bridge the broad gap between searching for enlightenment and actually attaining it. I welcome you to the journey!

Introduction

DISCOVERING *the* SOUL

*The final frontier in human knowledge
is the exploration of consciousness.*

Humanity has gathered an astounding amount of information on virtually every subject, and there is more information available today than at any other time in recorded history.
In fact, far more information has accumulated in books, in other
publications, and on websites than any one person could possibly digest in a lifetime. Nevertheless, some very basic questions
about the underlying mysteries of our existence remain unan-
swered.

This book is about perhaps the most important of those mysteries — the nature and purpose of the human soul.

THE SOUL OF THE MATTER

At some point, many wonder: "Do I have a soul? And if so, what
is it, where is it, what does it do, and what state is it in?" Perhaps
the biggest question of all is "Why can't we seem to see or even
find our soul?" Why isn't there more information about it?

Our society today offers very little guidance for how to

access the soul or how to utilize what the soul has to offer in daily life. Discussions of the soul by scientists and scholars, and even by many religious and spiritual teachers, usually have surprisingly little to say about how we can use and benefit from the soul's gifts. And yet most people believe they have a soul.

This lack of significant information explaining what the soul is and what it can do has long puzzled me. Over the years, in my conversations with clergy and spiritual teachers, I've usually found more questions and speculation about the soul than direct knowledge, and overall there is a lack of agreement over what the soul is and how it operates. If the soul exists, wouldn't such an integral part of ourselves be something we would all want to know more about? If we understood the soul, wouldn't that help us understand more about the nature of life itself — and where we're headed? If we could access the soul readily, wouldn't that help us successfully face some of the challenges that confront us individually and collectively?

In most cases, however, people don't seem to think about their soul very much. They accept that they have one, but they don't know how or try to use it.

TO BOLDLY GO WHERE
ONLY SOME HAVE GONE BEFORE

The final frontier in human knowledge is the exploration of consciousness. We access this realm through inner attunements, particularly through meditation. In other words, the answers to the questions we so urgently seek can be found within our own soul.

In fact, perhaps the most important aspect of the soul's subtle energetic presence is its ability to shift our consciousness to amazing and beautiful levels. When they connect with their souls, some people experience opening to enlightened states of awareness. Some have visions and dreams of angelic realms. Some feel a deeper communion with God, Spirit, or whatever name they give the underlying creative force of the universe, as well as with their own divine nature. Of course, many people all over the world are working toward these goals following many different paths. Whatever the path, I've found that awareness of the soul's presence can provide a dramatic help in achieving a shift in consciousness.

Yes, what's truly wonderful is that the soul's presence complements any other system of healing, clearing, or spiritual practice you may be following. It doesn't require you to adopt a particular belief system. I have experience with a wide range of healing practices — such as pranic healing in the yogic traditions, therapeutic touch, kundalini, Reiki, magnetic healing, shamanic healing, *shaktipat* (the energy transmission from guru to disciple), and the laying on of hands — and soul energy adds to and enhances any of these modalities or approaches.

The primary method in this book is a meditative process. Some see meditation as a contemplation practice that facilitates relaxation, while others see it as a prescribed set of postures, breathing methods, and recitations. I've practiced many varieties of meditation, and in the process I've developed a meditative attunement process that enables me to access areas of consciousness that aren't normally available through conscious thinking or analysis. In addition, I've found that I have an ability to assist others in discovering much of what has formed their life experiences, which allows me to help them improve their lives. Through the meditative processes you will follow in this book you will also be able to experience the transformational presence of the soul.

When I was taking science courses in college, I assumed that the field required scientists to be open-minded. While many scientists certainly are open-minded, most limit their speculations only to what they can empirically measure and observe. Thus, in a way, scientists limit themselves by the tools they use, and we will have to be bold at this phase in our human evolution to explore the soul and the realm of consciousness.

For scientists, a big part of the dilemma in describing and understanding the soul is that the soul isn't physical. Therefore it can't be measured through the physical senses or quantified using the usual scientific instruments or methods. That hasn't stopped some investigators from trying. In fact, more than one hundred years ago scientists tried to determine the weight of the soul by weighing people right before and right after death. Such efforts didn't meet with success.

Still, we're all aware that scientific understandings have themselves evolved over time, such as our understandings about how our solar system works and how, at the other end of the scale, atoms, molecules, and particles work. It would be naive to assume that there's nothing more to learn beyond what contemporary science has already explained. But it may be up to us to become the pioneers who take the first steps into the territory of investigating the soul's light and energy — at least until science catches up!

The purpose of this book and the soul-solution process is to allow you to have a unique and direct experience of your own soul through meditation and to begin to form a conscious relationship with it. Through this process, you will answer some of the most important questions about your soul, and it will enable you to integrate inner experiences with transformations in outer realities.

EXPERIENCING YOUR SOUL
BY ENGAGING WITH THE BOOK

Your soul is your own personal connection to the creative Source of the universe, which goes by many names, such as *God, Source,* and the *Holy Spirit.* Your soul already has the many wonderful and beautiful qualities we admire in the saints and respected teachers of all the world's great spiritual traditions. All the love, peace, kindness, generosity, compassion, joy, happiness, and bliss — the list could go on and on — are right there in your own soul. Since your soul already possesses these qualities, it stands to reason that as you deepen your relationship with your soul, these wonderful and beautiful qualities will emerge more fully in your day-to-day life.

But how to do it? How to draw closer to your soul so your soul's qualities can shine forth in all you think, do, and say? How to unleash the power of your soul so that you can bring healing to all the parts of you that need it?

Indeed, perhaps the most amazing aspect of all this is that awakening to the light of the soul doesn't require a special initiation or transmission from anyone. And when you think about it, why would it? This light is really the connection to your own soul, and it's fully available to *you.* What triggers the process is simply knowing about and actively acknowledging your soul. I've found that this process of acknowledging the light of the soul is all that's necessary to bring the soul's energy presence to the surface. The soul then automatically and naturally begins making changes in your life. And it knows what you need better than you do. As this beautiful inner light emerges, it helps you awaken and embrace the deeper spiritual truths within.

Like the light itself, this process of awakening has many names. Some call it an *epiphany*; some call it a *transcendental experience* or *enlightenment*. But what's remarkable to me is that, as astonishing as it is, it doesn't need to be regarded as something incredible or reserved only for the special, select few. This awakening is the most natural experience we could ever have, and it's available to *all* of us.

In *The Soul Solution*, I describe this process, which helps you nurture a new relationship with your soul, naturally allowing you to awaken spiritually and thus achieve the peace and happiness of living mindfully in the present moment, as embodied by the world's greatest spiritual teachers. This process also holds the key to the most miraculous healings you can imagine.

I suggest that you approach this book as a pathway into experience, rather than as a proposal for further thought or a useful collection of information. Its purpose is *experience*, not theory. The main method is a series of processes and meditations that allow you to have a direct experience of the healing potential of your soul right now, in this present moment, rather than hoping or wishing for it sometime in the future.

This isn't a one-time experience, either. Sometimes people have awe-inspiring soul encounters, and then don't seem to know what to do with them. In many cases, they may feel as if they lose the experience as time goes on. In this book, I will not only be showing you some ways to access the light of the soul, but will also guide you in how to keep it alive in your day-to-day life through ongoing practice. As you will see, there are many practical ways to apply the soul-awakening process to the challenges and concerns of day-to-day living.

Introduction

Your job is simple: Don't just read *The Soul Solution*; take the time to engage in the processes and meditations fully. The first time, you might just read the meditations to get a sense of what they're about. Then return to them, not once but several times; slow down and work with the meditations more deeply over time. If you do, all I'm promising will unfold naturally. All of this is possible through your very own soul. Welcome to the deep and rich awakening, the profound peace, the true enlightenment, and the amazing healing your soul has to offer!

EXAMPLES OF HEALING

Over the years, I've worked with many thousands of people using this subtle energy. The range of experiences people have with the soul is truly amazing. Some people have experienced virtually instantaneous healings of illnesses. Some have experienced an opening of extrasensory perception, and others have told me that their creativity and income increased dramatically within a few days or weeks after encountering the soul's presence. If I told you all that I've seen this soul presence accomplish, you might have trouble believing it. What I've witnessed convinces me that the soul is indeed one of the secrets behind miracles.

One person I taught the technique to described the healing effects on some of those she worked with:

Some wonderful results: One person has experienced relief of intense hip and leg pain that had been with her for a couple of years. Her quite noticeable limp is now almost gone. In another case, an anorexic who'd had trouble taking in adequate nutrition has now started eating twice a day and is also receiving intuitive messages about the nutrients she needs.

Another woman wrote of the joy she has experienced:

> I was at first waiting for [the soul energy] to come to
> me. Once I let go and just was, it sort of clicked into
> place, sort of like when you put a battery into position.
> It was like a groove that was waiting for the perfect fit of
> energy.... Then, instantly, when it clicked in place, tears
> of immense joy fell. It was a feeling of connection, like a
> pipeline to the Divine.

As these examples suggest, the soul is not just a healing energy
but a transformational energy that can deeply affect a person's
awareness and consciousness.

Most people I work with are very aware of the miraculous
energy of the soul filling them. Some see light, and others feel
vibrations. Some feel a tingling sensation, perhaps accompanied
by waves of energy. Yet others feel deeply relaxed while they
experience peace, euphoria, and bliss. As I see people filling with
this presence, I can watch the pure, divine light radiating from
them more and more brightly. This experience has helped me to
understand even more fully the many biblical accounts that link
spiritual people with light — light in these instances being the
light of the soul depicted in so many paintings of saints as a halo
or glowing aura.

People receive the awakening to their inner soul light and
learn to work with it very quickly, and they're changing their
lives in ways that many never imagined possible. The energy of
the soul has brought about significant relief, and even complete
healing, in the cases of people who've suffered chronic pain or
other conditions for many years. And it works for children, too.
As one eleven-year-old boy put it, "It makes me want to laugh!"

He was experiencing the wondrous feeling of euphoria that many have with such awakenings. Many adults have also described a feeling of exhilaration rushing through them.

Everyone has a soul, and everyone can learn to experience its many gifts. While such stories may seem miraculous, each in its own way, I don't want to imply that everyone will have the exact same experience. I've found that everyone is unique and responds differently. Some don't notice much of anything other than calmness and relaxation, while others experience dramatic changes. Everyone experiences the soul's energy and presence in their own particular way.

ENLIGHTENMENT AS AN ONGOING PROCESS

In my own evolution and in witnessing the unfolding of many thousands of others who've engaged with the subtle energetic presence of the soul, I've come to see that enlightenment is an ongoing process, not a destination. At each unfolding level of consciousness, the experience of life changes. For example, there are many ways for people to feel love, and we can experience love at various depths. We can describe each as love, but the actual experience can be significantly different from person to person.

This is also true of the unfolding of enlightenment. We associate an array of marvelous qualities with enlightenment: unconditional love, a sense of oneness, bliss, complete fulfillment, inner peace, happiness, emptiness, freedom, complete stillness beyond thoughts, and more. Some of these qualities may or may not be consciously present with the first enlightening experience. For instance, some people feel oneness and bliss in meditation, but they don't necessarily have their mind become permanently quiet with no uninvited thoughts. On the other hand, some people experience both potential aspects from the start.

Many people have had transcendent experiences of emptiness while meditating, but they may not have had their negative emotions dissolve once and for all; that state may come with future shifts. Some reach a certain level of awareness and stay at that level, while others continue to experience further awakenings. Certainly our personal commitment to ongoing spiritual practices, such as daily meditation, affects our progress.

In my personal work with thousands of people in workshops, meditation retreats, and one-on-one sessions, I've seen a wide range of people make shifts at all levels, so I know it's possible for everyone. Over the years, I've conducted more than twenty thousand sessions with people, helping them through their pain, struggles, and obstacles to achieve a deeper understanding of their true spiritual nature through connection with their soul.

As you continue through this book and practice the meditations and simple techniques I'll share with you, you'll discover that you too can drink from the spiritual source that gives rise to saints and spiritual luminaries. Using these simple procedures to draw close to your soul, you'll encounter the soul solution: the ability to unfold and create the life you may only have read about or dreamed about until now.

Note to reader: To download a free recording of the author reading some of the meditations in this book, use the code "SoulFilledHeart" at www.JonathanParker.com.

Part One

DEVELOPING *a* RELATIONSHIP
with YOUR SOUL

*I want you to be
everything that's you
deep at the center
of your being.*

— CONFUCIUS

Chapter 1

YOUR JOURNEY *to* YOUR SOUL

*Your soul has an ever-expanding capacity to open
and evolve, and it wants to rise to the surface
and embrace your life.*

In this chapter I'll introduce you to the first two of the book's meditative practices to help you connect with your soul. Over the years, I've developed a method of meditating with people in which I attune to their inner experiences to help them dissolve self-defeating patterns that create unhappiness. Anyone can use these techniques, and I always encourage people to be their own best teacher and guide. My role is simply that of a guide with some tools and resources to share.

One of the foundations of the processes in this book is *energy healing*, which is a method of mental and emotional clearing based on the concept that everything is energy, including all matter, thoughts, beliefs, and emotions. And your soul is uniquely suited to help you with this energy healing.

THE SOUL'S INVITATION

You begin your journey into your soul by thinking about your soul and wanting to know it better. Your soul has an ever-expanding capacity to open and evolve, and it wants to rise to the surface and embrace your life.

Even more than this, your soul has an ever-expanding capacity to open to, embrace, and evolve into something more than it currently is. And it's eager to share all of its gifts with you.

Everything in the universe, from the macrocosm to the microcosm, is in a state of motion. Everything is evolving from what it is at the present moment. You arrived at where you are now through this transformational process, and you'll continue unfolding, expanding, and discovering new levels of experience into the future.

What can accessing the soul help you evolve into? We can describe some of the qualities as boundless, fulfilled, beautiful, radiant, creative, generous, optimistic, eternal, free, light, timeless, flowing, soft, playful, harmonious, gentle, grateful, receptive, warmhearted, and more. The soul is capable of bringing you into a state of total integrity, mindful of the needs of others, nonattached, and yet deeply loving and caring, with a great curiosity and desire to expand the expression of all of its qualities.

The soul expresses all these and more wonderful qualities, which continually expand and unfold, leading to more goodness, more love, more caring, more compassion, and a greater capacity to give and share everything. Other qualities include joyfulness, openness, quietude, peacefulness, happiness, awareness, purity, innocence, and a sense of completion, satisfaction, and oneness with all that is.

Language is powerful in opening us up to experiencing the depths of the soul, which is why I'm specific in describing the soul's many qualities. In meditation, it's important to spend time with each of these qualities, as this helps to reveal more of that quality in our lives. Whatever stage of spiritual evolution a person is in, the soul already has all of these qualities, but we may not experience them since most of the time we're focused on our current emotional state.

The soul already possesses the state of being that's all anyone could desire. Thus, when we connect with the soul, we make it possible to bring everything we could possibly want into our everyday experience, while at the same time dissolving everything that we don't want.

In a real sense, we're *already* connected with our soul, and so we can know and feel the connection whenever we're attracted to anything that's beautiful, profound, creative, loving, peaceful, and fulfilling, whether in our interactions with other people, in our activities, or in nature. This aspect of the soul is reflected in the relentless pursuit of perfection often found among scientists, musicians, artists, athletes, writers, actors, and all others who seek to attain a high potential. So, in truth, the soul is present in human experience even when it isn't overtly recognized or acknowledged.

As we integrate the soul more deeply — and more consciously — into everyday life, more of the soul's qualities have an opportunity to emerge naturally. The challenge we often face in allowing the soul to become more present in our lives comes from how we choose to face the struggles and issues of our lives. Do we merge more deeply into the soul and fill each circumstance with the soul's presence, or do we give greater energy to the illusion of separation in order to preserve the costumes and identities we've assumed in life?

If we make a conscious decision to cultivate and integrate deepening soul realizations, we contribute to the evolution of our relationship with our emotions, our philosophy, our perceptions, our judgments, our reactions, and our spiritual state. As we discover more of the soul, we become empowered with dignity, integrity, and virtue. The soul exerts a comprehensive presence.

Although the soul certainly includes a transcendent aspect, connecting to it isn't just an escape into blissful transcendence. The soul is capable of being eminently practical. Part of the process of merging with the soul is recognizing that we're evolving beings. The soul knows what our own personal next step of evolution needs to be. Part of that evolution is the awareness that we're indeed transcendent beings, connected with and an aspect of the divine Source that created us. While each of us experiences our soul to different degrees, we can all experience our soul more deeply.

This may sound a bit overwhelming, but it isn't really — because your soul is your greatest resource, and it can help you take whatever the appropriate next step is *for you* as an individual. Your soul can bring oneness, wholeness, and completion to all areas and issues you may be facing. It has access to anything you're ready to accept and allow yourself to receive.

Our lives are part of a much larger continuum than our few decades on earth. As we understand this, we open ourselves up to the high calling and noble journey of cooperating and joining with our soul in its evolution.

You can learn to connect with your soul through meditation, and it gets easier the more you practice it. The more you apply yourself, the more you'll improve and the more benefits you'll enjoy. Don't be discouraged if at first you have only limited awareness of your soul. In my own case, I grew into an awareness of the soul and higher consciousness gradually, over time, as I persisted in my efforts. Ongoing practice and persistence are the key.

The first guided meditation, below, will take you on a journey to meet your soul. However, reading a guided meditation is different from listening to it, so it's important to follow a few basic tips: First and foremost, slow down your reading. Some people find it works best if they first read through a meditation at a normal speed to get a sense of it, then go back and, in a relaxed state, read through it *very slowly*. Keep in mind that the intention is to *experience* each moment fully. Consider pausing for a few moments at the end of each sentence to really take in the experience, and then pause a bit longer at the end of each paragraph.

What you'll get out of each meditation will increase the more time you take to experience it.

MEDITATION

Journey to Meet Your Soul

To download a free recording of the author reading this meditation, use the code "SoulFilledHeart" at www.JonathanParker.com.

Let's begin the journey to your soul. First, select a stretch of time when you won't be disturbed and don't have anything else to do. Silence the phone, and take care of anything else that might interrupt your meditation. Then sit or lie down as comfortably as possible.

When you're ready and settled, start with a comfortable, deep breath in through your nose. Hold this breath for just an instant before letting it gently out through your mouth. You'll notice that this starts a relaxation in your body, which enables you to begin letting go of the outer world so that you can put your attention on your inner world.

To help relax your face, separate your teeth slightly, and notice how your body relaxes a little more.

As you inhale, imagine you're breathing in golden light through the top of your head. Allow that light to filter into every muscle, organ, and nerve from the top of your head down to the tip of your toes. Breathe this light into every cell of your body.

Do this for two minutes, and put your attention on the light in the center of your chest, in what is known as the *heart and soul center.* Imagine a sphere of light like a miniature sun about the size of a baseball radiating golden light from your chest all through you and around you.

Keep breathing the light into your heart and soul center, as you continue relaxing and sending love to your heart and body. Allow yourself to deepen the process into your entire body.

Now tune in to the following statements, gently attuning them to your heart and soul rather than mentally analyzing them. Simply allow yourself to merge with the words and experience each statement within.

Say to your heart:

I send you all the love of my soul.

Say to your body:

I embrace you with all the love of my heart and soul.

Continue breathing in pure love and golden light. Fill your entire chest area with a radiantly glowing presence of golden light.

Allow the soul's love to merge into every muscle and nerve and to fill every cell. Allow this love to become part of every atom and molecule of your being. Sense the soul's love relaxing you and bringing a healing glow to your whole body, which spreads the radiant love outward all around you.

If there are any disturbances, distractions, or issues on your mind, say to yourself:

I ask the light of my soul to fill all my thoughts and feelings about these situations.

I send all my thoughts, memories, and feelings the pure light and blessings of my soul.

Allow your breath to be free and gentle. Feel a relaxed presence as you welcome the peaceful soul presence. Say to yourself:

I place my heart in the presence of my enlightened soul so that all may be healed.

I am willing to acknowledge my past and release it into the embrace of my soul.

I allow the source of love to embrace my heart.

I acknowledge the divine soul presence within me.

These statements are like prayers and intentions. They are requests of the deepest core of your soul, where all goodness dwells. You'll naturally and automatically receive a healing answer to your requests and intentions. Allow yourself to deepen into the feelings of receiving the love, light, and healing that live in your heart.

Allow yourself to receive the peace, gentleness, and love. Say yes to receiving peace, love, and healing, and ask them to deepen within you. Feel your heart saying:

I can trust my soul.

I can trust this process.

I can reach freedom, awakening, and enlightened states.

Each of these statements is a request and a prayer as well as an acknowledgment. Say to yourself:

I acknowledge my soul and the divine presence within me, and I open to receive infinite love and peace.

I welcome all the qualities of goodness of my soul, and I allow them to rest in my heart.

Drink in the soul's qualities, and say yes with thanksgiving. Let yourself deepen into these peaceful feelings. If you sense any tightening, questioning, or holding, bring the fullness of your request to the resistance. Say:

I surrender, release, and dissolve all my need for any resistance.

I surrender my heart to the fullness of the divine presence.

Beloved presence of divine love, help me to receive your presence more fully into my heart.

Follow your feelings, and whatever your experience is, return to your heart center and repeat:

I feel my soul deeply in my heart.

This helps to bring the soul and the divine presence to the place of need, and whatever is not an essential expression of the goodness of your soul will wash away and dissolve. Repeat this statement several times slowly, gently, and reverently:

I feel my soul deeply in my heart.

Deep in your heart, sense the presence of peace, love, and light that's being extended to you and that's emerging. You may see something visually, or you may experience the presence more emotionally or kinesthetically. Sometimes you may sense a deepening of peace and love, and other times you may simply feel relaxed.

Whatever you're experiencing, know that it's right for

you. There's no wrong way to do this. Allow yourself to deepen into your inner space and discover the gifts that are there for you. The key is to keep asking to open more deeply to receive the beauty, love, and light that are already awaiting you.

Continue requesting to open more deeply and acknowledging the soul deeply in your heart for as long as seems appropriate. When you're ready to conclude this meditation, take a deep breath, express gratitude, and fully connect with your body and surroundings. Slowly bring yourself back to being fully alert and aware.

GETTING TO KNOW YOUR SOUL BETTER

Every time you practice the Journey to Meet Your Soul meditation, you'll have an opportunity to strengthen your relationship with your soul. In the next guided meditation, you'll begin to get a sense of just how deep you can go as you get to know your soul better.

Remember that your willingness to practice these meditations over time increases your capacity to grow and evolve in relationship with your soul. Chapter 3 offers some additional guidance about creating an effective, soul-oriented meditation practice. As you experience the various meditations in the book and repeat them over time, remember that they build upon one another. As you continue with this practice, healing and an enlightened radiance will begin filling your life every day.

Also, note that several sentences in the following meditation use the word *God*, but feel free to substitute whatever word feels most comfortable for you to describe God or the creative heart of the universe. Other possibilities include *Source, the Creator, Nature, the Tao, Higher Power,* and so on.

MEDITATION

Deepening into the Soul Presence

Arrange yourself as comfortably as possible for this meditation. Pick a place and time when you won't be disturbed. Silence the phone, and take care of anything else that might interrupt your meditation.

When you're ready, start with a gentle yet deep breath in through your nose. Hold this breath for just an instant before letting it slowly out through your mouth. You'll notice that this starts a relaxation in your mind and body.

Say to yourself:

I feel the deep peace of my soul.

Repeat this sentence a few times with the intention of moving more deeply into peace each time.

Say to yourself:

I open to receive the peace of God and my soul.

Repeat this sentence a few more times with the intention of moving more deeply into peace each time:

I open to receive the peace of God and my soul.

Another soul quality is the certainty of being beloved by the Creator and Source of all. This means a feeling of knowing you're loved and you are love. A fullness, comfort, and warmth come with this awareness. Say to yourself:

I feel deep love in my soul.

I open to receive the deep love of God and my soul.

The soul has a wonderful lightness, purity, and softness.

Notice how you're now able to hold much more softly any issues that may have seemed strong and dominant, and how the feelings of lightness and spaciousness replace any struggle. Say these words to yourself:

I feel the lightness and purity of my soul.

I open to receive the lightness and deep purity of my soul.

When the soul is present, you'll sense a wonderful feeling of expansion, freedom, and connection with all creation. Sometimes that feeling is like floating on a cloud without a care in the world. Sometimes it feels wonderful, liberating, and blissful. These are some of the qualities that form the backdrop of what you experience when you integrate the soul into your daily experience.

Say these words to yourself:

I feel the freedom and expansion of my soul.

I open to receive the deep oneness with God and my soul.

I feel my soul deeply in my heart.

I feel deep, divine presence in my heart.

Deeper and deeper.

The soul has many other wonderful qualities, such as beauty, stillness, gratefulness, creativity, fun, happiness, caring, fulfillment, and so much more. Your soul is your personal resource for everything you could ever want or imagine. When someone triggers a reaction in you, such as judgment, anger, fear, or depression, the way back to peace is through reconnecting with your soul. The key is to let go of the need for your reaction or judgment and to open to receive your soul.

Say to yourself:
I merge into the pure light of my soul.
I bathe in the light of my soul.
I merge into the light of my soul.

Let the soul presence come into your being and trust the process. Be assured that the soul knows what it's doing. It is divine intelligence, so welcome it in. The soul already knows your needs, so simply open to receive the healing presence of your soul and divine presence. Be still now, and allow yourself to receive the gifts of your soul. Receive the presence of your soul and your divine essence into the depths of your being.

Think of the place where the angels are. Imagine and think of what that realm is like. Think of the love, light, and beauty. Think of infinite kindness and generosity. Imagine the joyfulness, happiness, lightness of being, deep peace, gratitude, and appreciation.

Imagine a place where all beings are in loving service to everyone. Feel the deep peace. Acknowledge the deep beauty that almost brings tears to your eyes. Imagine an all-encompassing caring and deep love.

If you can sense any of these qualities, you're feeling your soul, and by connecting with these qualities, you're experiencing your soul.

Your soul contains a richness of purity and deep love. No word in any language can adequately describe this experience. It's the purest and most beautiful creation you could ever imagine. Say to yourself:

I acknowledge and receive this.

The presence of this awareness is a refined, unconditional love that is all-pervasive. The fabric is light, and the essence is love. Words are inadequate to describe the incredible purity of the deep love that is the nature of your soul. The soul reveals an endless expanse of love and light as far as you can see, and that is your home.

You, your soul, and love are seamlessly one. Acknowledge this awareness, and invite it to dissolve the things that no longer serve you in a healthy or enjoyable way, such as any negative emotions, reactions, and thoughts. Negative thoughts are like old, worn-out clothing that you no longer have a use for.

The soul's underlying awareness is that everything in pain, struggle, and separation can be loved into dissolution because only love is real. You've entered the ultimate healing space. *Be* the love. This is who you deeply are. It's your true nature, and it spreads through all the levels of your whole being with pure beauty, love, and light.

Your soul blesses you with words of love, beauty, and joy written into your heart to enrich your realizations and bring more good things to you. Take a moment to drink this in deeply.

Express gratitude for what you've been given today. Make the internal request now to fully integrate all you've explored in this meditation, and allow this integration process to continue day and night until it's fully complete. You've requested to open to deep transformations, so as you have quiet time, feel into the subtle soul presence and acknowledge that it's always with you. When you've finished with this process for this time, be sure to acknowledge yourself and become fully present and grounded in the here and now. Slowly return to your normal waking consciousness.

Chapter 2

the SECRET of the MIRROR UNIVERSE

If something in your life isn't working the way you want,
you don't have to look outside yourself for the causes.

I n this chapter, we'll examine further why deepening your relationship with your soul through meditation can transform your life. A while back, I saw the actor and comedian Jim Carrey on the *Larry King Live* TV show. One of the things he said stuck with me: "I believe that everything that happens to you is the greatest thing that could ever happen to you. Everything — because that is exactly how the universe works. It gives you whatever you are in alignment with, and it's all designed to work on the weakest link you have."

This type of profound insight only comes from observing life closely, and I believe it's one of the most important insights a person could come to. Since life indeed seems to work this way, what, if anything, can we do to move things along so we aren't stuck forever dealing with our "weakest links"?

THE SECRETS OF MANIFESTATION

In his classic book *Think and Grow Rich*, Napoleon Hill wrote about a secret that many successful people have discovered:

People attract what they think about. In other words, we're like magnets, constantly attracting opportunities, people, and situations to us. Or, to put it in the terms of an ancient principle: Like attracts like. You attract and become what you hold in your mind both consciously and subconsciously.

On the surface, this insight seems to offer a simple solution to all the shortcomings we experience, since apparently all we need to do to be successful is to start thinking about success. But one of the biggest challenges of Hill's so-called secret is that what many people spend most of their time thinking about is what they *don't* want.

I often ask people, "What do you want out of life?" At first, this seems like an easy question to answer, but few people have really thought about it. So when I ask people, most pause and say something like, "I have to think about that, but I can tell you what I don't want!" And that's precisely the problem. People *attract* what they don't want because they spend most of their time *thinking* about what they don't want.

What Hill and others have called "the secret" is really not a new idea. Buddha once said, "All we are is a result of what we have thought." This is another way of saying that we are the creators of our reality. In order to better understand how this really works, we need to consider not only what we think but also what beliefs we carry at the subconscious level and, even more important, what we *feel*.

Yes, our feelings provide important clues about what we hold in our subconscious mind — what we *really* believe, deep down. Our feelings are the force behind the manifestation process. So what we focus on with our thoughts and feelings is what we tend to attract and create in our experience. To put it in terms of the oft-quoted biblical verse Job 3:25: "For the thing which I greatly feared is come upon me, and that which I was afraid of is come unto me."

When we realize that we draw to us what we fear, or what we focus on, it may at first seem like a negative scenario, but when we really grasp this fundamental process, it's actually quite empowering. As Joseph Campbell puts it on the DVD *A Hero's Journey*: "When you follow your bliss...doors will open where you would not have thought there would be doors and where there wouldn't be a door for anybody else,...and the world moves in and helps."

Rather than living with fear, if we can find a way to live with bliss, wonderful things open up for us. And bliss is readily available; it's just that most people haven't yet figured out how to feel blissful. Your bliss is not only a wonderful inner feeling that generates positive outcomes; it's also a natural characteristic of your soul. Yes, your very own soul is always happy, so when you're connected with your soul, you feel happy and often even blissful, and therefore your life is an experience of goodness.

When you've integrated the bliss, happiness, and goodness of your soul, you can easily manifest the wonderful results you want in your life because your thoughts, beliefs, and feelings have come into alignment and harmony with your true goals.

THE INVISIBLE MIRROR

Here's how the process works: Most people's thoughts and feelings arise in response to their immediate experience. Since daily life is full of little challenges, such as bills to pay, meetings to attend, and issues to solve, people become preoccupied with solving problems rather than with thinking about or experiencing happiness and success. As a result, they create experiences to match their conscious *and* subconscious thoughts.

Invariably, this leads them to experience even more challenges and disappointments.

If you want to know what you deeply believe, simply look at your life. It's a reflection in a perfect but invisible mirror of the beliefs you hold at the deepest level. Your mirror turns out to be your friends, your relatives, your family, your work, your talents, your possessions, your capabilities, your opportunities — everything in your life.

We've all heard the proverb "You reap what you sow," but most of us apply this concept only to negative situations. For example, we might say, "He wasted his life on gambling and alcohol, and now he's reaping what he sowed." But this proverb has a much broader application. It's far more than a warning about extreme or terrible consequences. Rather, it's a key to unlocking everything you could ever want.

The way this principle works is actually easy to understand: Life reflects what you hold at the deepest levels of your consciousness. This sounds simple, and maybe even obvious, but most people never think about it, and few live their lives as if it were really true. And yet, the very nature of life is that you get what you ask for!

This is why people of all faiths, praying to God by different names or no name at all, often have their prayers answered. If a call goes out with faith, belief, and the knowledge that God or the powers of the universe will answer, the sincerity, belief, conviction, and intention of the prayer cause a response according to the praying party's faith and beliefs. This is the nature of how life works. This is the way *everything* works: The universe functions like a giant mirror, sending back to you what you project into it with your thoughts, beliefs, and feelings — and the past patterns you've established.

The reason people often don't have what they want, or don't

get what they consciously claim to want, is that they have counter-programs running deep within them that broadcast the opposite intentions into the universe. The forces of your past feelings and beliefs put into motion the creative currents that orchestrate the circumstances of your life today. Whatever has been energized in the past will find ways to manifest in the present and future unless something is done to change what has been energized.

THE KEY TO CHANGE

When you finally realize that the universe reflects back to you what you've been holding in your consciousness at the deepest levels, your life will change. For one thing, if you really take in what this means, you'll do some deep soul-searching to uncover how you've created your own reality. Once you see this, you can learn how to create other realities.

Being aware of the mirror universe also encourages you to become much more mindful throughout the day because you realize that you're in the process of creation all the time. This is a crucial and profound understanding because it affects every single experience you have. This understanding reduces everything to a very basic process. If something in your life isn't working the way you want, you don't have to look outside yourself for the causes. This knowledge empowers you to create your life the way you want it to be. Can you see why this knowledge contains such tremendous power?

The universe contains all possibilities waiting to manifest, and it supports whatever you create through your inner beliefs and intentions. While many people continue to make excuses about why something isn't working in their lives, many others are busy achieving success with very nearly the same tools and circumstances. The universe responds to expectation.

Let's look at this a bit more deeply. Why are some successful, while others aren't? The source of some people's lack of success may not be immediately obvious. The subconscious messages being sent out to the universe may date back many years. Beliefs may be so old or deeply embedded that they seem to have no connection to current events. People may not believe they had anything to say about how they got where they are. They may think that they're merely victims of circumstance or bad luck, or that they were simply dealt a bad hand or were born at the wrong time to the wrong parents. Many people have had these types of thoughts, even if they don't express them.

Asking why you arrived where you are is important. Was it all blind chance, fate, or luck? It can be easy to think it was one of those forces, or to believe that you screwed up somewhere but now can't remember when or how. Rather than blaming yourself or external forces, you can instead engage the conscious and unconscious sources within you and shift or release the beliefs and patterns held there to change your life experience. Your soul is your ideal partner for this endeavor.

The mirror universe is the perfect system of justice and balance. The old saying "What goes around comes around" reflects an observation that goes back thousands of years. If your life isn't going the way you want, look inside; with the help of your soul, you can clear the patterns that aren't working positively and establish new beliefs and patterns that *will* work.

HOW TO WORK THE MIRROR
IN YOUR FAVOR

You may think that you'd like to be healthy, wealthy, and wise, and wonder why your life doesn't reflect those things. But how well do you understand why your life has unfolded the way it has? Does it seem as if many aspects of your current situation just emerged mysteriously?

Remember, you live in a field of potentiality that creates and forms itself according to your deepest thoughts and patterns, which you've set in motion in the past. While it may appear that many circumstances arise spontaneously, with no deliberate will or intention on your part, the truth is that it's your own consciousness that has made all the choices and decisions. Your will, beliefs, intentions, and desires impel creation and shape your experiences.

This means that your life as it is now has indeed emerged from the thoughts, words, actions, beliefs, and feelings you've energized in the past. Although thinking about what your life has been is a good start, it's also important to have an idea of where you want to go if you ever expect to get there. If you don't have that focus, then rather than living a life that is self-determined, you'll remain subject to the patterns of your past.

Only when you start to awaken to truths deeper than what your five senses reveal will you realize how you arrived at where you are today. Everything you think and do each day contributes to the stories you tell yourself about your life, which you subsequently find yourself living by, especially on a subconscious level. And the stories you tell yourself today are the scripts you'll live by tomorrow — unless you wake up and rewrite them.

This understanding definitely motivates you to be more mindful about what you think, say, and do. This insight keeps you attentive and wise, for you learn to observe what you're doing that creates what you don't want and to discover how to create what you really *do* want instead.

This process starts when you let yourself become quiet and still — as you do during meditation — and take your attention away from what you don't want and instead place it on what you want to experience.

Once you decide what you want, allow your soul to be an active partner in affirming and believing that you can have it, that you deserve it, and that it's possible for you. Your soul's natural optimism will help your belief at the deepest level that what you desire is in the process of manifesting in your life now.

You're not alone on your life journey. The greatest resource you have is your own soul. Your soul is there every step of the way to guide you through any challenges and obstacles you face. It's the metaphorical genie in the lamp that can help you create every form of goodness in your life that you can imagine.

Chapter 3

THE FIVE-PHASE PROCESS *of* SOUL MEDITATION

Mastery is worth any of the inconveniences
necessary to attain it.

I n this chapter, I lay out some basic principles about the form
of meditation I've found to be most effective in working with
the soul. There are, of course, many different approaches to
meditation. After years of study and exploration, I've identified
a simple five-phase process that works well for both beginners
and more advanced practitioners.

Committing yourself to an ongoing practice of soul-oriented
meditation is perhaps the most powerful action you can take
to deepen your connection with your soul and to enjoy all the
benefits your soul has to offer. To begin, you'll want to set aside
at least twenty minutes each time you meditate, and plan to meditate at least once a day. If you can do thirty minutes or more at a
stretch, or meditate twice a day, so much the better! What's most
important, however, is that you make meditation a regular practice, so choose a time frame you can commit to wholeheartedly.

Every time you meditate, be sure to select a comfortable
location where you won't be disturbed or distracted by phones,

animals, or other people. Settle into a peaceful place in a comfortable position that you can hold for the duration of your meditation practice. It's generally advisable to be sitting rather than lying down, as many people find they're more likely to drift off to sleep if they're reclining.

All the meditations in this book incorporate five important phases: grounding; centering with your awareness in your heart and connecting with your soul; attuning to your soul's guidance; integrating your soul experience; and expressing gratitude before returning to normal consciousness.

PHASE ONE: GETTING GROUNDED

The first process or phase of your meditation is to center and ground yourself. This helps you settle your energies, quiet your mind, and tune in to your inner realms. To meditate effectively, you want to relax physically, emotionally, and mentally, so let go of any outside concerns and focus your attention on the present moment.

Generally, some form of controlled or conscious breathing is helpful for this. For instance, measured breathing works well to settle your energies as you inhale and exhale to the same slow count from one to five, but any form of slow, connected breaths will create the stillness necessary for clarity to emerge.

Initially, spend at least five to ten minutes in this phase of your session, as it takes practice and patience to quiet the mind from the distractions of the day and turn your focus to spiritual and inner work. You may want to accompany your breathing with a soothing visual image, such as a quiet and restful natural setting near some calm water.

You can enhance your experience of grounding yourself by directing your intention to form a connection from the base of your spine to the center of the Earth. The visual image that I find works most easily for this is to imagine that you're sitting on a tree stump three feet in diameter, and the trunk of the tree and its roots go deep into the ground. It's important for the diameter of your grounding connection to be the same all the way to the center of the Earth. The first chakra is located at the base of your spine, and its energies move downward into the column of energy you have created with your intention. This grounding has a wonderful stabilizing effect on your whole being.

When you're well grounded, your thinking and memory improve, you're more focused, you feel more empowered, and you have more ownership of your space. When this happens, you aren't as affected by others, and you become more stable and balanced.

This grounding has two other important effects: First, it helps keep you in the present moment, and second, it gives a place for anything distracting to be released. We tend to pick up energies from other people, organizations, and even places we've been, and these subtle energies have an effect on our feelings, ideas, and reactions, which can interfere with the clear guidance of our soul. Have you ever noticed that when you're around people who are sad or depressed, you might find yourself starting to feel down? On the other hand, when you're around people who are enthusiastic or happy, you will find yourself energized. This is more than a psychological effect. A transference of subtle energy takes place among people who are engaged with one another in any way. The stronger the emotional content of the relationship, the greater the energy transfer.

Once you've established good grounding in your meditation, hold the intention to have it stay in place at all times. You'll find that this helps you throughout the day. In fact, if you turn your attention to it a few times during the day, you'll always be in a grounded state. Then, when you're in your meditation practice, it will take only a few seconds for you to turn your attention to your grounding and hold the intention that it remove and clear any energy from you that isn't yours or that doesn't fully support you.

PHASE TWO:
CENTERING YOUR AWARENESS IN YOUR HEART AND CONNECTING WITH YOUR SOUL

The second phase of your practice — after settling in, relaxing, and grounding — is to center yourself so you can establish your connection with your soul. Everyone's consciousness has a point of focus. If you pay attention to yourself right now, and scan yourself, you can become aware of where your awareness is currently focused.

Typically, your consciousness is focused on the area that is holding your attention. For instance, if you have a pain in your shoulder, you're likely to find your awareness focused somewhere near your shoulder. If your mind is active, your focus is probably somewhere in or around your head. If you're feeling stressed or tense, your focus may be in your abdomen or solar plexus. Consider the expression "What does your gut tell you to do?" When you're tuned in to your "gut feelings," your awareness is focused somewhere around your abdomen.

Another area where your attention can often be found is in your chest or heart center. This is where people carry grief, sadness, and emotional pain, as well as love and compassion. The chest area is especially important in meditative practice because the soul is most easily accessed through the greater heart-center area in the chest.

So, during the second phase of your meditation, put your

attention on your heart center in the upper center part of your chest, and reverently say to yourself, "I ask my soul to emerge in my heart." You'll also find it helpful to rest one or both of your hands over the upper center of your chest, as this helps you stay focused there, facilitating your connection with your soul. Sit quietly with this process for a minute or so, to allow yourself to connect with the words and your soul. You can repeat your request several times; each time deepens your connection with what the words represent.

Begin to notice and feel the awareness of your soul in response to your requests. At first, you may simply feel a quietness come over you, but over time more of a presence will emerge. You may also find it helpful to repeat other positive statements, almost like a mantra, such as "I feel my soul" and "I feel divine love in my heart."

The idea is to repeat something that helps you feel as if you're making an inner connection with your soul essence. As you repeat these statements for several minutes, you'll find yourself connecting more deeply each time. You'll sink more and more deeply into the experience of discovering your true nature, which is an expression of infinite love and light. Centering your awareness in your heart and connecting with your soul is a skill that improves with practice. Soon you will be in tune with the inner guidance of your soul nearly all the time, like a continuous inner communion with your soul throughout your day. You'll feel a harmony and congruity as you align yourself with the inner guidance of your soul, and you'll notice that you feel off track when you aren't aligned in this way.

Step-by-step, your old programs and beliefs will relinquish their control as you are increasingly guided by the inner direction of your soul, bringing healing to the parts of you that have lived in separation or fear. In time, your mind chatter will quiet down and no longer draw your attention.

PHASE THREE:
ATTUNING TO YOUR SOUL'S GUIDANCE

After you've centered yourself in your heart center and made a connection with your soul, you're ready for phase three of your meditation, which is attuning to the divine presence of your soul through the repetition of a phrase, a sacred sound, or a sacred name.

There are many sacred names, and many have an "ah" sound in them, which opens and expands the heart center. Examples include *Yeshua, Buddha, Yahweh, Allah, Abba, Amma, Adonai, Rama, Alleluia.* The phrase *I am* is also heart opening, as is the phrase *I feel my soul in my heart.*

Repeat the word, name, or phrase you've chosen slowly, reverently, and quietly every ten or fifteen seconds; your intention is to deepen the connection with your soul with each repetition. Call to the divine light and your soul to embrace you and merge into you. After a period of time — which can be anywhere from a few minutes to thirty minutes or more — you'll notice a shift. If you stay with this practice, you'll feel supported, comforted, and spiritually healed. At this point, compare how you're feeling now with how you were feeling — and what you were experiencing — before the meditation.

Your meditation itself will guide you concerning where and how to explore next. You'll be taught from within — by your own soul. Once you feel you've reached a nice state from the repetition of your word, name, or phrase, practice sitting in peaceful stillness, and attune yourself to the subtle impulses that arise. Be willing to stay out of judgment to allow new awareness to arise within you.

In the early stages of your meditation practice, you may not see, feel, or hear much of anything, and so you might think either that you're doing it wrong or that something within you is getting in the way. Neither of these conclusions is true. Judging yourself, getting impatient, or doubting yourself will only interfere with opening to deeper meditative experiences. Just about everyone goes through this phase, but it will pass as you continue with your daily practice. No matter how long it takes to open your receptivity, you'll succeed if you persist, and the rewards are well worth everything that you put into practice. Mastery is worth any of the inconveniences necessary to attain it.

If you find you're getting stuck in a particular meditative phase, it can be helpful to go back to the grounding phase and release negative thoughts through your connection to the center of the Earth. Then connect with your soul through your heart center and resume to repeating your sacred sound before returning to sitting in peaceful stillness.

PHASE FOUR:
INTEGRATING YOUR SOUL EXPERIENCE

The fourth phase of your meditative practice is integrating your experience before you bring yourself back to your normal, day-to-day world. In this phase, you simply relax your mind, let go of any questions you may have been posing to your soul, and become still. Sense and feel the peacefulness and state of expansion. You may want to rest in this phase for at least five minutes or possibly longer. Give yourself permission to merge fully and integrate your deepest soul truths into every part of your mind, body, and being.

PHASE FIVE: EXPRESSING GRATITUDE BEFORE RETURNING TO NORMAL CONSCIOUSNESS

The fifth phase of your meditation doesn't take long, but it's a true spiritual door opener. Simply express gratitude for your meditation session, regardless of your perception of its nature or quality. Gratitude is a form of surrender that opens you a little more each time you express and feel it.

Once you've expressed your sincere gratitude, reconnect your awareness to your five senses, and notice what you're sensing. Notice sounds, feelings, and other sensations. Take several deep breaths before opening your eyes, and savor the smells in the air and the feelings in your body. Relish the way you feel as you begin to stretch your body. Be mindful of not contracting or tensing at the thought of returning to your normal day. Give yourself permission to hold the shifted space of your meditative awareness throughout your day.

As you return to your normal activities, you may think you're losing what you've experienced in meditation, but know that your awareness has stretched from where it was to a new experience of yourself and your spiritual connections. As the day goes on, you may find that you flash in and out of the awareness you gained in your meditation. This indicates that you are, in fact, changing. Notice how the new insights live in the back of your mind throughout the day and give you a fresh experience of whatever lies before you.

The more you meditate and connect with your soul, the more you realize that your outer perceptions have limited and confined you and that the inner truths of love and light are beginning to emerge from within. Your awareness gradually awakens to further reveal your inner soul — and your core essence of love, light, and beauty.

Chapter 4

GETTING *to* KNOW *the* QUALITIES *of* YOUR SOUL CENTER

As you deepen your relationship with your soul,
you deepen a loving relationship with your life.

The real secret to working out your life in the best possible way is realizing that you already have exactly what you need to resolve all your challenges and to create and attract everything you could ever want. Rather than looking elsewhere, you need only learn to tune in to and utilize the most transformative and most spiritual resource you already possess: your own soul.

This chapter is about taking the next steps in getting to know the amazing qualities of your soul center.

YOUR SOUL CENTER

Your soul center is where you connect to the real you, which in turn is connected to, and one with, all existence. Your soul center is your personal doorway to connecting with divinity and the fullness of all creative power.

When you engage in this chapter's meditations, keep in mind something you'd like to manifest — which could be a quality as well as a thing. We tend to think of manifestation in terms of material goods, such as a car, a house, or money, but it's even more important to manifest the refined qualities that make everything else in life worthwhile.

What do I mean by *qualities?* Here are some soul qualities to consider: compassion; caring; kindness; gentleness; generosity with your time and resources; supporting others in need; unconditional love, acceptance, and trust; grace; nobility; patience; appreciation; gratitude; lightness of being; serenity; joyfulness; thoughtfulness; and a sense of humor that enables you to laugh at yourself and enjoy the fun of existence.

These qualities, among many others, are by-products of the soul becoming more of a presence in your life, and they can all be cultivated by putting your attention on them.

You make your connection with these qualities of the soul through the process of placing your attention on the heart area in the center of your chest, as described in the previous chapter. By attuning to your heart and your deeper feelings, you create a deeper connection with the soul centered there. This is quite different from listening with your ears and processing with your analytical mind, so it takes a little practice to get used to, but everyone can do it because everyone has a soul center.

Even while you're reading these words, you can get a sense of your soul center and all it has to offer. Simply move your attention to the center of your chest. As I suggest in the second phase of meditation outlined in chapter 3, put one hand over the center of your chest to help you deepen your heart and soul connection, and then relax into this comforting and peaceful presence.

As you gently move your awareness from your head to your soul center, allow whatever you sense to just be there, without forcing or judgment. The connection with your soul comes from an inner invitation and request to open yourself to it and allow it to emerge. As you sense or listen, or even read, from your soul center, you naturally access aspects of yourself that are below and beyond the mind — and beyond your personality and identity — because you're making a connection with your soul and essence.

WHO ARE YOU REALLY?

Because most people operate most of the time from their active mind and emotional self, they usually aren't aware of the soul's subtle presence and influence.

Your individual soul is your unique *essence*. The soul is the part of you that some have called the *divine presence*, the *higher self*, or the *inner guide*. It's the part of you that's untouched by your trials and tribulations, or even by your death, because it's an indestructible spark of the divine that observes your development and evolution across eternity.

Your soul supports your life, your mind, and your body, yet it exists beyond your mental and emotional aspects. Your soul is always moving toward greater truth, beauty, love, and harmony. It's what you see reflected in the sublime and refined qualities of sages and saints. Ultimately it's what opens you to universal unity and expansion of consciousness.

The soul's essential nature has all the most beautiful and refined qualities that anyone could ever want, and it expands like a flame, becoming brighter and brighter until it radiates like the sun. Since the soul is already complete, it's really only your experience of it that grows. The soul emerges more fully from within as you put your attention on it.

As your soul emerges more and more in your life, it increasingly radiates all of its qualities in you and through you. As you turn your attention to the place within where your soul centers itself, you progressively sense more of a rich and beautiful presence making itself known.

Your soul center in your chest enables you to access the spiritual being that you are, bypassing the illusions of the mind and emotions. You tune in by feeling and sensing in your body, rather than through thinking about the process, or questioning, or trying to figure things out.

Your soul center is your doorway to the love, acceptance, and healing needed by all the parts of you that have been struggling or that have been hurt — all the parts of you that have felt alone or have been discouraged. While your physical heart circulates physical nourishment to your whole body, your soul center circulates its spiritual essence and qualities through all parts of your being. The soul radiates its presence all through your body and energy field. It establishes its intelligence and the purity of its qualities all through you, and it allows you to create an intimate relationship with divine love and joy. The following meditation will help you deepen your sense of this.

MEDITATION

Deepening into Your Soul Center

As with all the meditations, select a time and place free from distractions and disturbances. Get yourself comfortable and breathe deeply. Allow your mind to relax. Gently bring your attunement to your body by moving your awareness from your head to your body, and especially to your chest.

Tune in to the feelings in your body. Place your hand over the center of your chest to help deepen your heart and soul connection. Move your hand around until you find a comforting place for it, and allow yourself to sense whatever is there. Sometimes thoughts or feelings arise as you do this, and other times you'll feel more peaceful. Just observe without reacting or judging as you deepen into the presence of your own body. Take a few minutes to notice, feel, and attune yourself to your inner space.

Continue to let your attunement focus on your soul center, and sense anything else you notice in your body. Let this be a natural and relaxed process that frees you from any self-conscious effort or *trying* to make something happen. Just gently tune in to whatever is taking place within you. Notice the peacefulness, quietness, and spaciousness, as well as any other sensation. Take a few minutes to feel into this part of the process.

As you settle into attuning to, sensing, and feeling your inner space, you'll discover a subtle peacefulness or resonance within your heart and soul center that indicates that you're deepening into your soul connection. As you connect with the subtle changes within, you'll automatically and quite naturally deepen into an awareness of the realm of the soul.

If your analytical mind tries to figure this out, relax it. This process of attunement is one of sensing and feeling, not thinking and analyzing. Just keep tuning in to your inner presence, with the desire to connect more deeply with your deep heart and your soul.

Let your attention and sensing be where your deep soul presence resides. You need not try to feel anything. This is a natural process of turning your awareness toward your inner presence. For instance, you don't need to understand meteorology to know what the temperature in the room feels like on your skin. Similarly, simply sense and feel your inner space and your connection with your heart and soul.

Just be present with the resonance within you. You aren't trying to hear or see anything. You are simply relaxing and opening to observe, rather than trying to make anything happen. Go slowly with this part of the process. Simply be present with what presents itself as your body becomes quieter and as your mind relaxes its attempts to question or control the process.

Your soul is always present and available. If you feel it isn't present, or that it's blocked, know that this is your mind's attempts to understand or control the process. Your soul is your inner resource. It's a presence that can soothe, resolve, and heal all your issues. It has a remarkable ability to wash away your limiting perceptions, myths, pain, and wounding. So just relax with your soul. There's no wrong way to do this process. Simply ask to connect with your own deep self, and know you can trust the process completely. Keep tuning in to your inner presence with the desire to connect more deeply with your deep heart and soul. Take a few more minutes to feel into this part of the process.

Your intentions are your keys to opening the door to the soul and all of its healing gifts, qualities, and resources. Be open to receiving the fullness of the soul's presence. Say the following to yourself slowly:

I give myself permission to receive and feel my soul.
I am relaxed, soft, and open to receive my soul.
I allow myself to tune in to my soul deeper and deeper.

I feel the comfort of my soul's presence.
I open to receive the presence of my soul.
I allow myself to feel my soul deeper and deeper.
I receive the healing gifts of my soul.
I feel the comfort of my soul's presence.
I love my soul.
Deeper and deeper.

Feel free to repeat any of these statements as many times as you sense would be helpful. If you find that one of the statements feels particularly helpful, repeating it many times helps you to deepen into the experience of it. Take a few minutes to feel into this part of the process.

By connecting to your soul deeper and deeper, you automatically and naturally open yourself to receiving the healing, qualities, and gifts of your soul. By opening to receive more, you automatically connect with your soul deeper. Say the following slowly to yourself:

I open to receive the presence of my soul.
My soul finds me.
I receive my soul, deeper and deeper.

As you connect with your soul, you'll find that it blends its qualities more and more into your life. You'll increasingly sense its presence more and more, and with that presence come the beautiful qualities of peace and love and beauty. Say the following slowly to yourself:

My soul merges into my mind.
My soul merges into my consciousness.
My soul seeks to connect with me deeper and deeper.
My soul wants to connect me with the divine.
I open to receive my soul.

I open to receive the divine.
I receive my soul, deeper and deeper.

Your soul is your source of a loving relationship with your life. Your soul connects you with divinity, where the source of all healing resides.

Sense your soul's invitation to merge with it. You've waited a long time for this to happen. Sense your soul's intention for you to have a loving relationship with it. As you deepen your relationship with your soul, you deepen a loving relationship with your life.

Your soul is a doorway to the Source of all, and your soul is intelligent and knows what you want and need. The natural openness and presence of your soul can heal grief, anger, fear, and sadness by merging its presence all through the areas of pain. If there's any special area of your body or your life that needs attention, invite your soul to embrace it now. Hold your attention on your need, while also holding the intention for the enlightened soul to merge into it. Take a few minutes to feel into this part of the process. Now say these words to yourself:

I welcome my soul to embrace my attitudes about my life.
I welcome my soul to embrace my childhood beliefs and conclusions.
I receive my soul.
I welcome my soul to embrace my judgments.
I receive my soul.
I welcome my soul to embrace my anger and frustration with my life.
I receive my soul.
I welcome my soul to embrace my body.

I receive my soul.

I welcome my soul to embrace my special needs.

Let this last statement be as specific as it needs to be. Gently let your awareness follow and merge into the process of your soul's merging into your special needs. Say these words to yourself:

I open to allow receiving the presence of my fully aware soul.

I welcome the presence of my enlightened soul.

As I listen for my soul's presence, I open to receive more and more.

My soul is my gateway to return to my divine Source.

I merge with my soul's unconditional love and healing grace.

Hold the intention of sensing your soul, then merging with it, and finally integrating it into your awareness.

When you feel ready to bring this meditation to a conclusion, bring your awareness into your body with the fullness, realizations, light, essence, consciousness, and experiences of the meditation fully integrating all through you. Express gratitude for all you've received.

Bring yourself fully into your normal aware state, fully into present time. Say to yourself, "I am fully alert and aware. Right here, right now." Feel deep appreciation.

COMING HOME

As you're beginning to experience in the meditations, your soul is your center of wisdom, power, and love. Your soul is what enables you to be present with what's true and to live beyond the projections and illusions of the mind. Your soul provides peaceful inner guidance about whether something is true and good for you or not because the soul isn't colored or affected by anything external.

Being connected with the soul's presence is a wonderful way to go through the day and live life. *Sensing* is a process of attunement, as you notice, feel, and receive a connection with the soul. With sensing, there's no struggle or trying; there's only observing and receiving. As you deepen your attention into your soul center and connect with your soul, you'll notice a warm, radiant presence.

Letting your feelings deepen through attuning to the inner presence is how you connect with the life force and soul essence. As you give up trying to connect, you sense that you already are connected with your soul and spirit. Your soul brings the awakening of deep wholeness, deep love, deep understanding, deep peace, deep joyfulness, and more.

Your soul is your source of inner strength and empowerment, and by calling to it and asking to connect with its deep healing and peace, you're liberated. In the next meditation, you'll get an even deeper sense of this place of liberation and peace that is your true home.

MEDITATION

Your True Home with Your Soul

Arrange yourself as comfortably as possible. Pick a place and time when you won't be disturbed or have anything else to do. Silence the phone, and take care of anything else that might interrupt you.

When you're ready and settled, start with a gentle yet

deep breath in through your nose. Hold this breath for just an instant before letting it slowly out through your mouth. Sense and feel the welcome relaxation in your mind and body.

Say the following slowly to yourself:

I receive my soul.

I receive deep healing and peace from my soul.

I love the embrace of the beauty of my soul.

Your soul is your source and offers the answer to reconnecting with the parts of you that long for a deeper fulfillment through unity with your Creator and with deep divine presence. Through your soul, you feel and realize your oneness with the intelligent and loving ocean of existence, and through your feelings, your soul communicates these realizations to you. Soften into receiving your soul even more, and deepen your sensing and intention to merge into the fullness of your soul. Take a few minutes to feel into this part of the process.

What you seek is already seeking you. Your soul is reaching through all dimensions into your heart to express itself through your life. Your desire for deepening your spiritual connection is evidence of this fact. The divine presence of your soul, which is the real you, is connecting with you through your desire to experience your spiritual nature. This is a natural and automatic process that your participation accelerates.

As you hold the intention and desire to connect with and merge with your soul, you'll notice a change in the atmosphere around you. You may sense this as deepening into stillness or as a deepening calm. You may sense it as a spaciousness and expansion. You may also feel it differently each time you turn your attention to it.

Hold your intention unwaveringly to merge more deeply with the intelligence and presence of the divine light of your soul. Think of your soul as the spirit of God, Source, or Oneness within you, and the light and mind of God bringing you a miraculous, light presence. You'll find this presence transforms and keeps transforming until its qualities of happiness and peacefulness manifest in your life. This is your true, deep home, which feels more like home than any home you've ever known. Feel welcome in the hominess, comfort, and satisfaction that are your soul. Take a few minutes to feel into this part of the process.

Your home is with the soul, and it fills you with peace, freedom, lightness, and love. Acknowledge this and feel into these gifts and express gratitude for them. Take a few minutes to feel into this part of the process.

As you connect with this presence a few times a day, or more if you can, even if for only a few minutes, you'll find that what previously shook your world will have little or no power in your life. Your temperament, demeanor, and inner space will take on an assurance, an empowerment, and a presence of calm love because these are what your soul offers you and brings to you.

Realize that God's intelligence underlies all manifestation. It flows through all life, and in truth, the intelligent life force we call the divine presence makes possible everything wonderful. When you're attuned to your soul, every step you take, every word you say, and every thought in your mind is the divine soul presence within you operating through you.

As you acknowledge this presence, everything you set your mind to manifests beautifully and wonderfully, for this is the nature of the soul's presence. Through the recognition and use of this beautiful soul presence, you can bring any and every wonderful quality into manifestation. As you acknowledge the sacred presence within your soul, the higher self, the divine self, God within, and the spirit of love and life all emerge more fully and fill your life with their wonderful presence. Say to yourself:

I call my soul to merge into all resistance and unknown blocks.

I allow my soul's wisdom, insights, and intelligence to merge into my body, mind, and being.

I give my full permission and power to my soul to manifest my every good desire.

I receive a steady stream of purity and love flowing into my life and my creations.

I bathe in the waves of light filling my body and flowing into every cell.

I receive the soul's infinite love, peace, and purity.

As you conclude this meditation, express gratitude for all you've received. Now, take a deep breath and be present in your body. As you return your awareness to your body and present time, you may notice you feel different. Of course, this is just perfect, for the new you is present with the radiant light of your soul. Stay attuned to this presence as you continue with the rest of your day.

Part Two

MOVING *beyond* FEAR and the EGO

Knowledge is the antidote to fear.

— RALPH WALDO EMERSON

Chapter 5

the SOUL SOLUTION

When you remove false perceptions and illusions,
your true self remains, and you automatically experience
more love, beauty, harmony, and happiness.

The idea that we create our own reality — that is, the concept of the mirror universe, which I discuss in chapter 2 — often seems to ring true, but it also raises some troubling questions. Sometimes it's easy to see this principle at work in our lives, but other times, especially when things aren't going very well, it can be hard to understand how we set certain events in motion.

Of course, we don't have as much trouble with the concept when things are going wonderfully — for example, when stock prices are up, or we get the contract we were hoping for, or when our health is good. It's fairly easy to take credit for the good things, but when our health falters, or when financial problems come up, or when our relationships are in trouble, we wonder what happened!

In many cases, people claim they've tried everything imaginable to change things, and yet nothing changes. The reason for this is that most of the forces sustaining reality are below conscious awareness and therefore aren't known or recognized. We have accumulated wounds, habits, and belief patterns that are embedded in our body, mind, brain, and subtle energy system. And since we typically don't remember when or how an issue or condition got started, we may wonder why undesired events ever manifested in the first place.

But once you discover and understand the source, all the mystery is resolved. In part 2, we will look more closely at this source, which comprises all the false aspects of ourselves that get in our way. I will also describe my three-step soul solution, which entails removing everything you're not — the fears, the core patterns, the struggles of the ego — in order to reveal the truth of who and what you are. As your soul becomes more present in your life, you'll feel an inner happiness and radiance that you may have experienced only briefly before.

IDENTIFYING FEARS AND CORE ISSUES

Almost every problem we encounter in life is based on some form of fear. The energy of fear can locate itself in any area of the body and create physical and emotional symptoms. As you clear the fear, the conditions often clear up, but unless you eliminate the fear at its root, simply treating the symptoms will only cause the mind or body to create other symptoms. This often happens with certain therapies that only address the outer condition without also clearing the underlying causes.

If, however, in addition to treating the symptoms, you also release the subtle energy that's causing the symptoms, and shift your consciousness with regard to the underlying issues, the mind and body can return to a state of healthy balance. The energy meridians then open so that the life force can start flowing again, and this causes the body's chemistry to start working in a healthy way. Ironically, our difficulties can be gifts that reveal where we need to bring healing and where we're ready for growth, but first we need to get to the root cause, which I call our *core issues*.

Most of us struggle with core issues. Core patterns appear when we struggle with circumstances over a protracted period, or when we experience a period of growth. Core issues have a powerful impact on all aspects of our life. They carry strong emotions, beliefs, and reactions. When you clear core issues, you become much more empowered to create what you want.

Common core patterns center around issues and emotions such as terror, hatred, fear, anger, worry, feeling unworthy, self-doubt, thinking something's wrong with you, feeling unlovable, feeling trapped with no way out, feeling helpless and hopeless, experiencing deep feelings of aloneness and abandonment, and others.

When an event activates a core issue, you may feel devastated. You may feel as if your life has been crushed, or you may be frozen in fear, extreme confusion, deep depression, or a sense of abandonment. You may even feel physical pain, such as tension or a sensation of gripping in the chest or solar plexus. You may be overwhelmed and controlled by the core pattern.

In most cases, core issues accrue over a lifetime and remain deeply embedded unless or until we address them. These issues touch us at the deepest levels, and they aren't cleared quickly, as much as we might like it to be that way. Indeed, while the soul solution I offer is designed to help resolve core issues, I also suggest you seek out someone you can talk to directly. Shifting or clearing a core pattern can be difficult on your own. For help dealing with core issues, many resources and professionals are available, including psychotherapists, psychiatrists, marriage and family therapists, bodyworkers, hypnotherapists, energy healers, spiritual counselors, and others.

The challenge with core issues is not the experience or event that triggers them, but the emotional charge that gets attached to them. For example, post-traumatic stress disorder (PTSD) occurs when people keep reacting to a trauma years after an event; they carry the emotional charge and keep re-experiencing it emotionally. They may have frequent flashbacks to the event, and at the very least they experience strong negative emotions associated with the original event.

The same thing happens with a core pattern. The strong emotional charge connected to the pattern keeps the reactions alive. If you've experienced terror and deep fear in your solar plexus, or if you've ever had a deeply broken heart where you felt pain or agony in your chest, these experiences activate core patterns.

Fortunately, when you manage to release a core pattern, your whole life changes because you also release a tremendous amount of disturbing energy. This frees you from the tyranny of a lifelong problematic pattern.

THE EGO'S ROLE IN CORE ISSUES

How can you tell if you're dealing with a core pattern or simply a challenging issue? Core patterns are manifestations of the primary issues of the ego. The *ego* is the aspect of yourself that develops over time, and it is separate from your soul and your divine reality. The part of you that you naturally think of as *yourself* is often the personality, which develops from birth onward. The personality is formed from the traits you acquire from your parents and from your experiences. Underlying the personality are many subidentities with traits you've carried over from your past and maybe even many lifetimes. This collection of subidentities is composed of your past and current beliefs, preferences, and emotional reactions and is what constitutes the ego.

The ego is driven by many defenses to protect itself from whatever it perceives as a threat to its security, comfort, or existence. Many of the traits that you may think of as being fundamentally human are actually defensive characteristics of the ego. These include emotional reactions, beliefs, judgments, criticism, and blame. The ego relies on survival strategies to cope with the many threats that it perceives due to its sense of separation. Although all people have similar reactions and defense mechanisms, each person develops a unique style and preference for particular defenses. But whatever the defense mechanism, the underlying core mechanism of the ego is fear. The ego is responsible for all core patterns.

For instance, the ego utilizes the defense mechanism of fear to keep us from danger. This may sound like a good thing, except that most people are driven by fears that have no real basis, and by holding on to these fears, they generate the energies that can create or attract the very thing they fear. This is the mirror universe at work.

The ego's perceived separation from our divine Source engenders a vast number of fears. Because the underlying reality of our existence is really love and light, the experience of separation isolates the ego in darkness and void, and the ego will do anything it can to prevent itself from feeling the terror of this pain. At the core of the fear is the ego's terror of being annihilated or banished forever into the depths of separation. Typically, people aren't directly aware of these deep fears. Instead, they experience them indirectly, such as through fear of the future, a generalized anxiety, or fear of the unknown. All these unconscious fears make up the core issues that we need to address.

As mentioned above, the ego's defensive strategies also include a range of emotions — anger, rage, worry, guilt, hatred, depression, futility, powerlessness, helplessness, hopelessness, victimization, intolerance, arrogance, and stubbornness — as well as using the mind to judge, criticize, and blame. To keep from feeling the pain of insecurity and separation, the ego drives us to seek attachments through needing, wanting, possessiveness, control, endless searching, feeling that there's never enough, and continually looking for external things to bring a sense of fulfillment or completion. Though of course, they never do.

By systematically reducing and eliminating these core patterns, you can expand your awareness to a greater realization of who you are as a being of light and love.

THE CORE OF THE CORE

Imagine that you're like a thousand-watt lightbulb buried under a pile of dirt, which represents the many layers of the ego. Little light, if any, would shine through, but as you clear away the dirt and debris, more and more light would shine forth and radiate out all around you. Everyone, whether consciously aware of it or not, is in the process of discovering what some refer to as the *true self.* This is really just another name for our *higher self* or our *soul.* While I sometimes use these terms interchangeably, my preference is to refer to our true core as our *soul.*

The true self or soul is the real you under the cloak of your many personality traits, subidentities, ego traits, and core patterns. Under them all is the very pure, wonderful, loving, and radiant being you were created to be. This deep part of you is always aware of its connection to the divine Source of love and light. It's present with you now, at this very moment, but it normally operates below your level of conscious awareness.

Each person is unique and yet similar. We all have a human body, which is largely the same, but we each recognize our own many small differences. One essential similarity among everyone is that we all have a soul, and we're all made out of divine love, so we all have the same inherent beautiful purity, clarity, and deep nature of love that composes our true core.

Not many people experience their soul on a regular basis because the ego gets in the way. The ego, or *ego-personality*, as many refer to it, has many of the characteristics we associate with our distinct and unique self, including our emotions, judgments, and reactions. But this *false self* is not who we really are, and it usually lives with varying degrees of pain, struggle, and suffering.

The soul lies beneath the surface of our awareness most of the time because the ego has surrounded us with layers of illusions stemming from our mind, our senses, and our perceptions. Living in separation from our true nature causes all of our problems and makes our core patterns seem so intractable.

When you're free of fear and connected with your soul or divine nature, you're far better able to deal with all of life, including anything that may appear to be threatening. Once you're free of fear, such things rarely if ever come up.

THE THREE STEPS TO FREEDOM

The soul-solution process has three basic steps: First, identify the underlying patterns that are causing your problems; second, acknowledge that the patterns are *not* your true self and disidentify from them; and third, engage in a clearing process in which the love and light of the soul dissolve the patterns. Let's look at the steps one by one.

THE FIRST STEP:
IDENTIFY THE UNDERLYING PATTERNS

First, it's crucial to identify the underlying patterns that are causing the pain or struggle in our lives. Every effect has a cause. As we've already seen, what you have or don't have in your life didn't materialize by sheer chance. It had a cause in a deeply held, possibly subconscious belief or pattern in yourself.

What causes you to have an experience you don't want? Mental and emotional patterns are at work causing your reactions, many of which you're probably unaware of. Again, you know that you have pain or that you're struggling, but you may have little idea why. I've found that around 80 percent or more of the causes of problems lie beneath a person's conscious awareness. These are the blind spots that can be difficult to clear without help. After all, if you don't know what the cause is, how can you clear it?

Remember the inscription "Know thyself" at the Temple of Apollo at Delphi? Wise words and sage advice, but while theoretically simple, it's often easier said than done.

The first part of the soul solution is to spend some time in self-examination to determine the underlying forces causing the conditions in your life. Since we typically manage to clear only what we've discovered and identified, this is a crucial step.

To do this, you must go beyond coping skills or procedures that only treat the symptoms, and address the underlying energy patterns and belief structures that support the difficulties. Through the soul-solution process, you'll learn to dissolve the source of the problems; this is the focus of the meditations and exercises in parts 2 and 3 of the book. Each time you clear a layer, the old reactions continue to diminish, until eventually they're gone forever, and you become a transformed person. As you transform and clear your consciousness, the causes of pain, suffering, and struggle vanish. The result is a life of deep peace, love, and happiness.

When the consciousness becomes cleared of core patterns, amazing results can occur, not just with emotional and psychological issues, but with physical problems as well. Even serious medical conditions can sometimes go into spontaneous remission. Of course, someone with a serious physical condition needs to follow whatever appropriate medical steps are necessary to treat the condition. But by also clearing the underlying subtle energy causes, you dramatically increase the chances for true and lasting healing.

In the end, *healing* from the point of view of the soul solution is more about a transformation of the consciousness that underlies our troublesome conditions, whether they are physical, emotional, mental, or spiritual.

We all have the ability to uncover the causative factors that create our lives. It's important to look at a wide variety of possible factors as we explore the underlying causes of conditions, including ancestral patterns, belief structures, past-life patterns, patterns in the subtle energy systems, genetic factors, karmic factors, inner-child issues, traumas, patterns in the brain, patterns in the subconscious, and patterns stored in the body tissues. In addition, we need to consider the patterns in the subtle bodies, including the etheric body, causal body, chakra system, and aura. This covers a lot of territory, which explains why time is necessary to uncover the causative factors thoroughly.

This is all part of the first step of identifying the causes of the condition. This step is perhaps the most important part of the process, and the one that requires the most time and attention, since many of the causes are buried. It takes careful attention to attune to your inner space to discover all that needs to be cleared.

The Process of Self-Discovery

The first step requires introspection, as if you were a detective seeking out the subtleties of each issue or pattern. One of the challenges is to avoid the mind's relentless proclivity to examine, analyze, and project conclusions. The discovery process is felt as well as analyzed. The most effective approach is to tune in to the nature of the inner experiences first, before trying to think about, categorize, and define them.

We've all learned to rely on the analytical mind so heavily that we tend to experience our lives and ourselves almost solely through descriptions and definitions. Some people are totally descriptive and don't relate to visualizing or intuitively exploring their inner landscapes, but most people fall somewhere along a continuum between vivid visualizations and detailed descriptions. With practice, we can develop more fully our intuitive and visual perceptions, and this is important to do, for all the ways of gathering insights are useful in soul-solution work.

Tune In to Self-Talk: One way you can receive impressions about the causes of your core issues is by tuning in to your subtle inner voices, or what is known as self-talk. You undoubtedly already hear the messages of your inner voice much of the time, but trying to listen to them is a bit like having several radios on simultaneously. Everyone's mind is nearly always chattering away, but as you refine your inner-listening skill, you'll find yourself better able to derive important insights from your beliefs and the core of your reactions. With practice, you'll learn how to filter out the noise and discern important self-talk clues into the underlying beliefs, needs, and emotions that you want to clear.

Receive Information Kinesthetically: Another important approach is to receive information *kinesthetically*. This means sensing or feeling what you're experiencing. Sensing what a pattern feels like and where you feel it is a helpful source of inner information and a vital part of the soul-solution process.

When I began exploring these subjects more than thirty years ago, I couldn't see anything except a dark gray field in my meditations, visualizations, and inner explorations. In addition, I didn't really understand what people meant when they asked me what I was feeling. I wasn't aware of what I was feeling internally, and I wasn't even aware of my self-talk. I wondered what was wrong with me because I kept hearing about people who could see, hear, and know beautiful and wonderful things, and all I was receiving was a field of gray. I wasn't hearing anything other than my own mind's chattering. I finally refined my ability to discern what was operating inside, and I discovered specific insights that were helpful both to me personally and to my work with others. What I'm explaining in this book can save you a great deal of time and concern.

Identifying Patterns

When you're dealing with a mental or emotional reaction, start with your physical feelings about it. Most people tend to focus on intellectualizing or verbalizing their situation, with such thoughts as "I feel unworthy. I'm not good enough. There must be something wrong with me. I feel stuck."

A good detective gathers evidence before drawing conclusions, and that's what I suggest here. If you start by analyzing, the mind becomes erratic; it's easy to seamlessly slip from one current of thought to another, and your conclusions won't go as deep or be as thorough. Instead, start by tuning in to your body and its physical sensations.

Exaggerate the Feelings in Your Body: One helpful technique to get clearer is to *exaggerate the feelings* in your body. If you're feeling a clenching sensation in your stomach, tighten it more. If your hands feel tense, squeeze them tighter. If you're discouraged, drop your shoulders and slump. If you exaggerate the physical state, the associated emotions will usually become more noticeable.

Ask Questions: If you find you're not wanting to address a negative situation or feeling, ask yourself, "Why not?" Asking questions about what you're experiencing is an important part of discovering all you can about the issue so that you can release all of it. The more you discover about a pattern, the more of the pattern you'll be able to release.

Tune In to Sensations: Thoughts produce emotional states, and beliefs also set up emotions, which are then felt in the body. For example, the thought "I'm not good enough" can lead to sadness, which may then be felt in your abdomen.

Sometimes the sensation is subtle, while at other times it may be fairly strong, but because it has persisted for so long you have probably gotten used to it, and therefore don't pay much attention to it. As you experience challenges, relax and tune in to your body. Feel how the sensations present themselves in your body. The feelings could manifest as a tight shoulder, a contraction somewhere else, a nervous feeling, or a headache.

Let the physical aspects show themselves, then explore them and describe them in words to yourself. Tell yourself what you're noticing. This helps you to be more specific about the conditions and will enable you to be specific in releasing them when you get to that part of the soul-solution process.

Tune In to Emotions: Next, tune in to the emotion. If the emotion creates a tightness in your body, is it tight as if it's mad, tight as if it's afraid, tight as if it feels out of control, or tight as if it's in stress? Feel the emotions. Once you feel the emotions, memories may surface, and then the self-talk starts to show itself: "I'm sad, mad, hopeless, depressed, afraid, lonely."

In response, ask yourself, "About what?" Then continue by inquiring about whatever else the self-talk wants you to know. In this part of the process, your task is simply to explore and to gather as much information as you can about what you're experiencing.

THE SECOND STEP:
DISIDENTIFY FROM THE UNDERLYING ISSUES

After the first step, or discovery phase, of the soul-solution process, the second step is easier. It involves first acknowledging the pattern or issue, and then recognizing that it's not your true self and that the soul didn't create it. This process is called *disidentification*. You acknowledge the pattern, and then acknowledge that it isn't you. It isn't the real you, but rather only an aspect of the false self or ego, and, therefore, it can be dissolved, let go, or transmuted. This may seem obvious, but it's nonetheless important to acknowledge.

Ego-Defense Release

Reactions and core patterns manifest and are stored in several ways. Usually, physical, emotional, mental, and subtle-energy components accompany them. Ultimately, all reactions and defenses are rooted in the ways the ego defends itself.

Identify Specific Traits: The ego is like a computer virus or program that has invaded everything you think you are. The ego corrupts your connection to your soul and keeps you from getting the results you would like. To remove this invader, it's very helpful to discover the programming in each place it resides so that you can release it. Identifying specific traits is important, since the more specifically you identify them, the more specifically you can release them when you get to that stage of the soul-solution process.

Remember, the driving force of the ego is to protect itself, under the guise of protecting you. The ego feels unsafe and insecure, so naturally it strives for security. The most effective way to deal with the ego is to recognize that it's suffering and in pain and wants to go home to find healing, completion, and comfort. It has searched for rest for a very long time and is doing the best it can to protect itself and you, but nonetheless it's lost and unable to find peace. This is where you come in with your conscious mind, awareness, and relationship with your soul and inner truth. You already have what the ego is looking for.

Treat the Ego as an Injured Child: An effective technique in working with the ego is to treat it as a person you love who's experiencing painful struggles. Suppose that person is your child. How would you be inclined to treat the child? Think of the ego as that injured little child who keeps hurting him- or herself over and over. If you regard the ego as a sentient being, you'll find you're able to have compassion for it the way you would for an injured child. Feel compassion for the part of your ego that needs to defend itself. Approach the ego with the intention of wanting to help and heal it. It is much more skillful to view the ego this way than to treat it as an enemy to be overcome with force. A combative approach won't succeed very easily. The ego is well practiced at defending itself against such attacks, and it will dig its heels in deeper and find a way to survive.

From the ego's point of view, it has performed a service of protection for you, and it won't relax and let go unless it knows it is completely safe and no longer in need of the defenses. The way to reassure the ego of this is to approach it with mercy, compassion, and a desire to relieve its suffering, and perhaps even with understanding and gratitude for its efforts in protecting you.

Express Appreciation for the Ego: Having gratitude for the ego may seem like a stretch at first, but it's a very useful strategy. When you reach the awareness of appreciation for the ego, it will relax and release because you'll no longer be resisting it. The way to experience gratitude for the ego is to acknowledge that it has done the best it could to help you survive and arrive at the place where you can recognize you no longer need it. Now that you have discovered your soul and the soul-solution process, the ego can be freed to release its need to defend itself. The ego's traits will then loosen their grip and let go. The process may be thought of as surrendering and letting go without judgments and expectations about results; however, being patient and having a positive sense of expectancy are helpful.

The Importance of Disidentification

Releasing the ego depends upon your ability to allow it to release by letting go of everything holding it. You do this by simultaneously acknowledging it while disidentifying from it with a recognition that it's not the real you.

Reframe Language: It's also helpful to reframe your experience by shifting the language you use. Change such statements as "I feel angry, afraid, or depressed" to something like "The ego feels angry, afraid, or depressed." This shift in perspective helps you let go of owning the experience or letting it own you.

Release the Helium Balloon of Core Patterns: Another way to think of dealing with your core patterns is to focus on the image of holding a helium balloon in your hand, opening your fingers, and letting it fly free. Once you've released it, the balloon will lift off on its way. You don't have to throw the balloon into the air or teach it how to rise. The same is true of the ego. As you let go of your *need* for it, it releases its grip, lets go, and effortlessly disappears. The key to the release lies in observing and recognizing the process taking place without putting effort into making it happen. Throughout the process, your role is as a detached observer. In other words, you explore the nature of the reaction without becoming swept up by it or engaged in it. Otherwise, you risk identifying with the ego's feelings and become engaged with them and consequently unable to release them. Because the ego cannot release itself from itself, ego-based methods have very limited utility or effectiveness, if any.

In a sense, the ego is trying to evolve out of the trap of going from one painful suffering circumstance to another. The ego is actually trying to find its way back to love and completion, but it can't do it on its own. Your role is to allow it to have its freedom by no longer holding on to it as if it were you and you need it. This is the process of disidentification.

THE THIRD STEP:
LET THE SOUL DISSOLVE THE ISSUES

After disidentifying yourself from the core issues you have identified, you're ready for the third step in the soul-solution process. In this clearing stage, you engage the love and light of your soul to dissolve the issues and patterns. The meditations in the remainder of the book will give you plenty of experience with the clearing stage. This process works with physical, mental, or emotional issues, as well as with spiritual blocks and limitations.

When you remove false perceptions and illusions, your true self remains. As your soul surfaces, your mind begins working in a very different way, and you automatically experience more love, beauty, harmony, inner strength, gentleness, and happiness.

You can do the entire soul-solution process on your own, but working with another person often proves helpful. This is because many people have difficulty finding the patterns that control their lives, disidentifying from them, and then clearing them. So it's helpful to find kindred spirits who can support you on your life journey and perhaps point out your blind spots.

Because this information is so important to your understanding, to end this chapter I'll give you a summary of the three steps of the soul-solution process, which you'll be drawing on in the meditations in the rest of the book.

RECAP OF THE THREE STEPS OF THE SOUL-SOLUTION PROCESS

1. ***Identify the Underlying Patterns:*** Identify the underlying problem, pattern, or issue, and determine its causes. This is a process of self-discovery and entails getting an awareness of both conscious and subconscious causes. The introspection entailed in this self-discovery can be the most time-consuming part of the process. Feelings, sensations, and self-talk can provide clues to underlying beliefs and fears that provide the underpinnings of the problem.

2. ***Disidentify from the Underlying Patterns:*** Acknowledge the problem, pattern, or issue, and then recognize that it isn't your true self and the soul didn't cause it. This process is called disidentification — a recognition that

the problem isn't the real issue but only an aspect of the false self or ego.

3. *Let the Soul Dissolve the Patterns:* Allow the love and light of the soul to clear and dissolve the problem, pattern, or issue. When you remove false perceptions and illusions, your true self remains, and you automatically experience more love, beauty, harmony, and happiness.

Chapter 6

the FEAR FACTOR

The truth is that the past is nothing more than a memory,
and it has no real existence other than what we project on it.

During the thousands of private consulting sessions I've done over the past thirty years, one of the most common themes I've encountered is fear in one form or another. As I explained in chapter 5, the primary drive of the ego is fear, so it makes sense that fear would underlie most of the issues people bring up when seeking counseling. The ego is motivated by fear of the future and fear of the unknown; it fears it will be destroyed by some unknown force, and so it creates an almost endless list of defense mechanisms for protection. In this chapter we'll look at fear from a spiritual perspective, and I'll give you an experience of how the soul-solution process can help you move beyond it.

If you type *fears* into an Internet search engine, you'll discover that there are more than a thousand different fears and phobias. Just a partial list of these fears demonstrates the many varieties and serves as an education in itself. I found nearly one hundred fears listed under the letter *A* alone. Two well-known examples are *agoraphobia*, a fear of being in crowded, public places such as markets and shopping malls; and *arachnophobia*, or fear of spiders, which even inspired a Hollywood movie of the same name. Other entries under A are less well known and include *achluophobia* (fear of darkness), *agatephobia* (fear of insanity), *amathophobia* (fear of dust), and *anuptaphobia* (fear of staying single).

From this simple taste of the thousand-plus fears, you can imagine how extensive and how detailed the whole list is! And the fears and phobias found on such lists don't even address the most common anxiety disorders, such as generalized anxiety disorder (GAD), panic disorder, and post-traumatic stress disorder (PTSD). Any one of these fear and anxiety disorders can become so severe that people lose their jobs, experience severely impaired relationships, or wind up in the hospital.

Some of the basic fears I've encountered in working with people include worry and uncertainty about the future, fear of change, fear that something bad will happen, fear of making a wrong decision, fear of making a mistake, fear of getting hurt by others, fear of a circumstance repeating itself, fear of being controlled by outside forces, fear of being taken advantage of, fear of failure, fear of rejection, fear of loss, fear of pain, fear of intimacy, and fear of being a victim.

In addition to fears people are conscious of, people often describe themselves with language that reveals underlying fear, even if it's unconscious. Such terms include *directionless, timid, self-conscious, anxious, lacking in self-esteem, tense, defensive, rebellious, insecure, shy, apprehensive, cautious, embarrassed, jealous, vulnerable, self-doubting, self-questioning,* and *guilty.*

Fear can also reveal itself in negative expressions, such as: "My life is chaotic." "It's not my fault." "Life is a struggle." "I can't handle life." "It's hard for me to forgive myself." "The world is scary." "I don't feel safe." We humans have countless ways of expressing the pervasiveness of fear in our lives.

In one of the all-time most famous quotations about fear, President Franklin Delano Roosevelt said in his first inaugural address of March 1933: "The only thing we have to fear is fear itself — nameless, unreasoning, unjustified terror which paralyzes needed efforts to convert retreat into advance." This powerful statement still rings true, but what Mark Twain said puts it in perspective: "I am an old man. I've had many problems in my life. Most of them never happened."

With fear so prevalent and debilitating, it's important that we find an effective way to treat it. To be certain, some fears are viewed as beneficial and are generally seen as healthy because they keep people from danger or lead to positive results. For example, some would say that a smoker's fear of developing cancer is a healthy fear if it causes him or her to give up smoking — the danger is real, and the fear can lead to constructive steps.

Other healthy fears include those that generate survival behaviors when we're faced with dangers, such as taking evasive maneuvers to avoid an auto accident, coping with a natural disaster, or surviving an attack by a wild animal. Of course, in these cases, fear becomes destructive if it paralyzes appropriate action.

And then there are the fears that are considered irrational (which is the definition of a phobia). These are unhealthy fears of harmless situations, such as *auroraphobia* (fear of the Northern Lights) or *aulophobia* (fear of flutes). Even fears of things we can do nothing to avoid, such as old age or nighttime, are fears that serve only to make people unhappy.

THE ROOT OF FEAR

Today many fears seem woven into the very fabric of our society, such as fear of terrorism, fear of epidemics, fear of a bad economy, fear of commitment, and fear of losing a job, as well as fear of being separated from people we love, fear of loved ones dying, and the all-encompassing fear of the future.

Many of our present fears are rooted in what Buddha called *delusions*, which are distorted ways of looking at ourselves and the world around us. Most fears also appear to be based on *illusions*. An *illusion*, as I'm using the word, refers to faulty interpretations and conclusions the mind makes about real or imagined circumstances. But if we learn to deal with the mind that creates the fears and to reduce and eventually eliminate the delusions and illusions, our fears themselves can likewise be diminished and in many cases eliminated.

If a fear has some rational basis, one obvious step is to take action to change that basis — for example, quitting smoking if there's a fear of getting cancer. Avoiding real dangers is a way of dealing with some fears; for example, avoiding a known violent person, not crossing a busy street without a crosswalk, or not flying in an airplane during a major storm. Of course, such fears can become exaggerated to the point where they become phobias that prevent people from engaging fully with life.

Nevertheless, most of the issues people have shared with me over the years haven't concerned real threats. Rather, they're rooted in some form of anxiety that arises from projecting ideas about what *might* happen or *could* happen, but that may not even be likely to happen. These kinds of fears include "What if" scenarios. But why fear what hasn't yet happened or may not even be likely to happen?

Such fears have their roots in the ego and its endless fear of annihilation. Generalized anxiety may also relate to a pattern set up in the subconscious mind, perhaps relating to childhood, heredity, or even an energy pattern transferred from a parent or ancestor.

WHAT TO DO ABOUT FEAR

Whatever the source, fear is abundant among human beings. It isn't worth blaming yourself for having anxiety and fear. You aren't alone in experiencing them. But you do have the ability to release them. The ego will always signal you about the next thing that needs release.

To discover what this is, use the techniques I describe in the first phase of the soul-solution process (in chapter 5), particularly paying attention to your bodily sensations and self-talk. Being attentive to reactions coming to the surface presents you with tremendous opportunities for growth.

Start by observing your thoughts and feelings because they are clues about what you need to release. Catching yourself while a reaction is happening isn't always easy, but if you pause a few times during the day and ask yourself what you're experiencing, your answers will indicate what you need to release and clear.

I suggest you stop what you're doing every hour or so if possible, and tune in to yourself and ask: "What have I been experiencing during the previous hour?" This is a helpful process that enables you to become more mindful as well as to discover what issue or pattern to bring to your soul-solution process. One way to help you remember to do this is to carry a small, inexpensive electronic timer in your pocket, and set it to vibrate every hour. The vibration is your reminder to check in with yourself. After a few weeks you'll find that you're automatically more mindfully aware all the time.

As you tune in to your body, let yourself sense the feelings. Then recognize that it isn't the real you causing these reactions and feelings — in other words, begin the second phase of the soul-solution process, disidentification. You might approach this disidentification process as if you were watching a movie of someone experiencing the same fear or anxiety. Observe yourself and your patterns as if you were a character in a movie. Later in this chapter, you'll also see how the third phase of the soul-solution process applies — bringing in the energy of your soul.

WHY WORRY ABOUT WORRY?

Worry and anxiety are among the most common forms of fear. But with all the techniques out there to deal with fear, and with none of us wanting to feel fear, why does fear remain so prevalent?

One reason many techniques don't succeed in completely eliminating our fears is that they don't always address the causative factors that extend beyond the conscious and subconscious minds. Fear not only operates through the conscious and subconscious minds; it also exists in subtle realms of consciousness.

For example, a fear can be held in various layers of the aura, in what is sometimes called the *emotional body*, or it can be caught in one of the chakras. You and your ancestors created these thoughtforms of fear out of survival defenses. Every time you experience any form of fear, these feelings feed subtle life-force energy into the fear thoughtforms, which further sustain them. This not only energizes the thoughtforms but reinforces the fear responses throughout your body and consciousness.

Fear can sometimes seem like having another person living in you. In such instances, the fear functions like a subpersonality or subidentity, which possesses the qualities of the type of fear it holds. When it presents itself, it can surprise you because you might not feel it until a situation triggers it, when you might say to yourself, "Where did *that* come from?"

Another type of fear involves "waiting for the other shoe to drop," which is a negative expectancy about the future. The collective consciousness of humanity still seems to view life as a never-ending struggle. Amazingly, even those who seem to be above and beyond this perception are nonetheless influenced by it in some respect. Even those who have a lot of money may have areas where they feel lack — a subtle fear pattern — whether in the arena of health, relationship, or general happiness.

All of these kinds of fear are part of the ego-identity, and ego fears aren't usually cleared and eliminated by traditional psychological processes. To remove these kinds of fear, you need to use processes that create a true shift in consciousness, and the soul provides the solution.

THE ILLUSION OF THE PAST

Another way fear expresses itself is as a belief that the past is somehow true in the present. For example, if you've lost money on an investment in the past or made a foolish mistake, you might fear similar experiences in the future. As you will see, however, this is a hasty conclusion based on a faulty assumption.

The truth is that the past is nothing more than a memory, and it has no real existence other than what we project on it. We benefit greatly when we no longer treat the past as a determiner of our present or future. This doesn't mean forgetting your past — the past provides wisdom that can help prevent needless pain and suffering — but it does mean letting go of the painful aspects and struggles of the past. You can begin this process of release by tuning in to any uncomfortable feelings the past is creating in the present and stating an affirmation, such as, "I release and let go of the painful feelings I am feeling about my past."

Making such conscious statements of release sets your inner intention, which you'll then want to follow with a healing approach. The healing approach that most effectively deals with fear is the *way you live life itself*. Connecting with your soul and your deepest core truth is perhaps the most powerful thing you can do to live your life in a conscious manner. But don't let this become just another idea or belief! Let it be a realization that fills your consciousness and awareness as an actual, felt experience; you can do this by regular meditation with your soul, as you do when practicing the meditations in this book.

A SPIRITUAL SOLUTION TO FEAR

All people contain a quality of true goodness — the higher self, the indwelling divine essence, the *soul*. When you're in touch with and remain connected with your inner presence of love, peace, and goodness, natural laws will bring more love, peace, and goodness into your life.

To get another taste of how this works, place one of your hands over the center of your chest and rest it there. Get in touch with the soothing feelings that emerge naturally. Say to yourself, "I feel deep inner love and peace." If you repeat this to yourself several times for a few minutes while keeping your hand on your chest, you'll begin to experience the inner peace I'm talking about. Once you have a good connection with this peaceful inner presence, ask this soothing, healing presence to merge into and wash away any negative feelings. With practice, you'll be amazed at how well this simple process works.

ENCOUNTERING FEAR
ON OUR SPIRITUAL JOURNEY

Spiritual seekers go through several stages as their spiritual practice progresses.

The first is the stage of excitement and fascination, which is mostly driven by the desire to accumulate information. The discovery of new revelations can feel a bit like falling in love. We might find ourselves devouring books and going to workshops and retreats to seek answers, hoping for spiritual experiences and realizations.

The second stage of our spiritual journey is when we begin to realize that the reality beyond the five senses is the ultimate truth. Many of the religious ideas we grew up with give way to a higher order of spirituality that leads to a desire to merge into oneness. This desire culminates in a process where we merge with our soul and divine nature. This stage is often filled with a fascination concerning saints, masters, angels, and gurus, along with thoughts about transformations of consciousness.

In the third stage of our spiritual journey, the deeper truth arises that the only way to experience the highest states of consciousness, spiritual realizations, and the unification of consciousness is through letting go and detaching from everything the ego is. This includes letting go of everything we think we are and thought we wanted.

At this point, some part of us may hang on to the idea and importance of retaining a sense of self, even while knowing that it's all an illusion. This push-pull is what brings about a kind of terror. We might think, "I want to let go of the ego and merge with the divine, but I'm afraid to let go that deeply. I'm afraid to plunge into the unknown and lose myself." This creates an instant recoil from the shift into self-realization.

But if we manage to surrender the fear and terror, something amazing and wonderful awaits us in the fourth stage of our spiritual journey. This is the state of oneness and a full realization that we are actually all there is. This is beyond an intellectualization of the concept, and even beyond oneness. It's a full immersion into the realization of all there is. This state is impossible to put into words, so giving it a name doesn't begin to describe it, but it seems to satisfy the mind to have something to grasp. We only arrive at this point through a total and deep surrender of everything we think and everything we are.

This brings us back around to the subject of fear, since there's a point in any long-term meditation practice or spiritual journey when we have to go through the terror of the third stage in order to reach the fourth. This type of terror happens as we move into the areas of consciousness that lie beyond the rational and subconscious mind. Once they move through this phase, most people encounter the most profound peace and fulfillment possible. The soul-solution process to help you remove fears can help you navigate such terrors and reach the other side of peace, as well as help you with more ordinary, "garden-variety" fears.

MEDITATION

Moving beyond Fear

To download a free recording of the author reading this meditation, use the code "SoulFilledHeart" at www.JonathanParker.com.

Choose a time and place to do this meditation that will be free of distractions and disturbances. Arrange yourself so you are as comfortable as possible. When you are ready, begin with a full breath in through your nose and exhale gently out through your mouth. Allow yourself to get relaxed, and breathe deeply. Reflect on how fear exists to keep a person safe; it does this by creating emotions that drive a protective response. At this very moment, you're probably not generating fear, but the structures of fear are still there. As soon as you feed energy into them, they're triggered, and you start generating fear energy and the accompanying chemical response in your body.

Most fears are felt and processed in the third chakra, which is in the upper area of the abdomen near the solar plexus. Put your attention on your upper abdomen now. This is your center of fear, anger, and judgment. For this part of the process, get in touch with any tightness or discomfort you might notice there. This is a gentle process. With your attention on this region, ask yourself the following questions softly and audibly:

What do the sensations in my abdomen feel like?

Do I feel soft and open, or is there some contraction and tightness?

What would the sensation in my abdomen want me to know?

If this area of my body could speak to me, what would it say?

What thoughts and memories come to mind as I put my attention here?

What other insight would be helpful for me to be aware of at this time?

Relax, and give yourself some time with this process. Observe any shifts that take place in your body or your feelings when you say those words. Notice any twinges or pulling anywhere in your body. Observe and perceive anything that comes up when you repeat these questions to yourself:

What do the sensations in my abdomen feel like?

Do I feel soft and open, or is there some contraction and tightness?

What would the sensation in my abdomen want me to know?

If this area of my body could speak to me, what would it say?

What thoughts and memories come to mind as I put my attention here?

What other insight would be helpful for me to be aware of at this time?

Now you can also name any specific fears that you know you have by completing the following sentence:

I feel fear of _____.

Observe any internal shift or reaction as you name your fear.

Next, hold the intention of addressing the core of all the fears that live in you. Use these words as guides, and make them your own:

I know fear has protected me in the past.

I now know I no longer need fear.

My soul gives me all the protection, safety, and help I need.

My soul keeps me safe, so fear is no longer needed.

I now give myself permission to release fear and let it go.

I give myself permission to release fear.

I surrender and release all need to hold on to fear.

I surrender and release all resistance to releasing fear.

I surrender and release all fear of letting go of fear.

I feel filled with the light of my soul.

I ask my soul to completely remove, erase, and dissolve the core existence of fear.

I ask my aware soul presence to fully merge and integrate into all fear.

I now fill myself with the light and love of my soul.

Your request and intention make all of this happen. Regardless of what you are consciously aware of, a response to your requests occurs. Try to sense the sensations behind the words. Make the following words your own:

The conditions and circumstances that created fear are no longer present or needed.

I have found my soul, which keeps me completely safe.

I forgive myself and others for their part in creating fear.

I now bring all fear into present time — right here and right now.

I surrender and release everything that is not real in this present moment.

As you inhale your next breath, breathe love and light deeply into your body and guide the love presence into the places and spaces where fear has been living and say:

I bring in the pure love of divine presence.

I bring the pure love of divine presence into the core of the need for all fears.

I call to my divine presence and my soul to merge the fullness of love and light into the core of all causes of fear.

Now relax, surrender, and receive the answers to all your requests, and notice that internal shifts occur within you simply by making the requests and being open to receive. Keep requesting that love, light, and your soul presence fill all the areas where fear has been held, and simply observe and receive the experience.

Sometimes the ego will say it's ready to let go, but when you start to let go, it holds on, so repeat your intentions once again:

I receive the pure divine love, light, and presence of my soul.

I receive the pure divine love, light, and presence of my soul deeply down into the core source of all fear.

I now give myself permission to open and receive the healing light of the soul.

I open, receive, and trust.

I now create and implant love and trust into my full body and being.

I merge with pure, unconditional love and unconditional trust at all times, day and night.

Relax into a space of integration to allow all the words and intentions to deepen within you. Express gratitude for all you've received. Bring all the feelings and realizations with you as you bring yourself peacefully back to your normal state of awareness for everyday life. Sense and see the divine around you. Sense, acknowledge, and be grateful for the beauty and divine presence in you and around you.

Chapter 7

the END of the EGO

When you enter a state of willingness and openness
to having your consciousness shift
to embrace the light and unity,
it will happen spontaneously.

We've now looked at a number of key aspects of the ego and how it keeps us trapped in fear. It sometimes seems as if people endlessly attempt to clear issues, patterns, and problems from their lives, but end up circling around in spirals of recurring patterns because they don't go to the source where all patterns originate.

Many people experience a restless energy inside that generates a sense of incompleteness, as well as a deep, accompanying loneliness. This pattern also makes it difficult for them to go into the deep heart and find the soul and divine nature that's there.

RETURNING TO THE SOURCE
OF THE PATTERN

Most of the patterns and issues people experience can, as I've shown earlier, be traced to the origin of the ego. The development of the ego begins the moment people become identified as a separate, individualized existence — separate from the state of oneness.

The ego perceives itself as distinct from the unity state, alone in a universe of eternal separation. Existing alone in a universe of its own creation, the ego can't hope to find solutions to its pain, suffering, and isolation. And it can't see outside of itself to find the unity of love, light, and universal intelligence that's always there. Instead, the ego vainly and frantically keeps trying to find answers inside itself. But it will never succeed because the answers don't exist there.

The problem the ego faces is that it doesn't even recognize that it's separated from the reality that underlies all existence; it doesn't even know that there is anything outside of its own experience. It just knows that it's incomplete. Left alone and fearful of its self-created existence, it's filled with fear, dread, and hopelessness, often just barely masked over by the trappings of the personality.

As we saw earlier, the ego remains terrified of the prospect of dissolving into nonexistence — or the so-called *death of the ego*. Human suffering has its roots in this dread the ego feels, even when it gets attributed to external factors. All our troublesome feelings are produced by the ego's cast of created identities and subpersonalities driven by survival instincts. This is vital knowledge because, with this understanding, you can begin to disidentify from the subpersonalities at the same time that you're in touch with their beliefs and are experiencing the emotions they generate.

Language can't begin to adequately describe the ego's isolation, but adding *deep* as an intensifier before each adjective helps: *deep* isolation, *deep* dread, *deep* fear, *deep* abandonment. This same ego is the backdrop to just about every experience of every lifetime, supported and sustained by the energy that comes from deep inside us. Life with it is painful. We feel cut off from everything wonderful, beautiful, and loving. This accounts for the human condition of suffering.

FINDING FREEDOM FROM THE EGO

Given how I've described the ego, no doubt you'd like to be free of it! The soul, as I've described it, with its connection to the divine Source of love, happiness, and peace, sounds much more enticing. You may wonder how the ego exists inside, trapped in its isolation, when the soul is always there, open and present, feeling connected and at one with the Creator and the creation. How can they live side by side and not know each other?

Without going into a lengthy creation story, I'll simply say that at the moment of wonder at the threshold between light and dark, we find that a person can see both ways. This is much as it was with Janus, the Roman god of doorways and beginnings, who had two faces, one that looks ahead and the other behind. We, like Janus, can see God in one direction and the universal void of separation in the other. How do they exist simultaneously? They exist this way in conditional consciousness only. In the deeper reality, even the void is encompassed by God, or Source, and no separation as such exists.

The void is like a cell of consciousness floating inside the universal light of awareness. In the void, we're unaware of the light. But once we know this and see how it all began, we can begin moving out of the darkness and separation.

As souls, we start in oneness with the Creator and creation and feel completely absorbed in that presence. Then we enter the state of wondering what's in the other direction. The first thing we notice is that there's less and less light, and we move into darkness. As we enter the void created by separation from light, we're encapsulated in fear, and the fear plunges us into further separation. The deeper we go into the void, the more we experience isolation, and a shell of fear builds up around us — the fear of the ego.

From a deeper perspective, it simply isn't possible to be aware of isolation and separation while being aware of the light and unity consciousness at the same time. When you only know the void and the realm of the ego, you're subject to the physics of that reality.

But now you have the opportunity to enjoy a multidimensional awareness, and with this realization you'll find that the void isn't as large or as formidable as it at first appears. It actually gives way to light, since it's finite in nature, even if it doesn't seem that way when you are identified with it. When you're in the ego universe, it appears vast and eternal. But when you rise out of it, you see how it's really just a small encapsulation constructed from a limited view of reality.

With this insight, you can be aware of the void and shift out of it so that you can see light, and then realize that light is everywhere. All it takes is a *choice* to ignore the light, and then all you can see is the void. But with another *choice* you can open to the light of the soul, which brings light to all the areas that are caught up in suffering and fear.

ADDRESSING THE DEFENSES OF THE EGO

One of the most common subpersonalities of the ego is the archetype of the warrior. A warrior acquires or gains things by fighting and conquering, so when we want to attain or acquire something — like a car, a house, a job, a relationship, or a successful business venture — we think a price must be paid, but not just in time or money. Caught in the warrior archetype, we feel we have to conquer a challenge or subdue an enemy to obtain what we desire. In addition, some part of us may fear we don't really even deserve what we want. So we engage in warrior-style struggling, fighting, and suffering to pay the debt of being undeserving.

These underlying patterns have their roots in the past, often in how our parents treated us when we were young. Really, it goes back even farther, to the original separation from unity consciousness, because that's where all problems got started.

In any case, no matter how much we acquire, when we're in the domain of the ego, we never feel complete. It's like having an insatiable hunger. With this emptiness inside, we feel as if something's missing, and we conclude that something's wrong with us. We come to believe that we can only have anything if we suffer enough. Others oblige our invisible contract of needing to suffer by taking advantage of us in some way. It's necessary to neutralize these contractual provisions in order to free ourselves from feeling it's necessary to suffer out of guilt for having something we don't feel we deserve.

What follows is a clearing process that will enable you to surrender this and similar patterns.

MEDITATION

Surrendering and Releasing

Make all of your normal preparations for meditation by selecting a comfortable setting and eliminating any disturbances. Now settle yourself comfortably in a position for meditation. Take a moment to arrange yourself so that each and every part of your body is loose, free, and comfortable.

Adjust yourself so you don't feel any pressure or binding anywhere, and give yourself permission to become relaxed.

Settle back with a deep breath, and as you exhale, just relax. Imagine you're floating safely on a cloud as if you don't have a care in the world. Slowly take another deep breath in through your nose. Hold it for a moment, and when you feel comfortable, release it slowly and gently out through your mouth. Feel yourself relaxing more and more deeply.

Now repeat these words to yourself:

I now surrender and release all need for suffering and struggling.

I now surrender and release all need for fear and guilt.

I now surrender and release the need for thinking I'm undeserving.

I now surrender and release the need for feeling burdened by my past.

I choose to surrender and release this all now.

I receive the lightness and freedom of my soul.

Repeat these words several times, and make them heartfelt. As you do, you'll notice that you feel lighter and freer. In fact, you may feel as if you've been released from prison, and you hadn't even realized how much weight and burden you'd been carrying around. You may just have known that something was wrong and that life was a struggle.

Now it's time to move out of the darkness of separation and into the light. It's time to let go of the ego's sense of separation and living in an ego-centered void. By simply stopping what you're doing long enough to invite the light of the soul back in, you'll begin to feel the emptiness and suffering melt.

The soul's inherent nature is completion. The soul is complete, and any incompleteness you've felt is just an illusion. As long as you're groping in the dark, you'll keep bumping into things. By moving into the time before you turned away from the divine light and into the illusion of separation, you can re-create your history and neutralize the karmic trail of all your lifetimes.

It's time to surrender even the minutest part of you that has any curiosity or longing for what separation offers. If even a minuscule part of you desires separation, you'll be pulled into it. But once you've gone into separation and then fully come out of it, you know both sides of existence, and you can choose and commit always to live in the light, love, and oneness, and never go into separation again. This is an initiation of bringing the full awareness of the light, the soul, and God or Source into human experience, and erasing the *experience* of the void, but not the memory of it.

Let yourself take the necessary time for the transition from an ego-based life to a soul-integrated life. Look at the choices you made and the process that pulled you to make your choices. And let it all go. Surrender all aspects that want to attach through wants and desires. Be aware of the energy of the unlived life and the part of you that wants just one more taste, just a little more power and control.

Now it's time for release. Moving fully into the light of the soul takes complete letting go. Trying, struggling, and straining are functions of the ego. But when you enter a state of willingness and openness to having your consciousness shift to embrace the light and unity, it will happen spontaneously.

Face the darkness with the truth of you, and notice the light dissolve the darkness. The light of the soul is bright, strong, and comforting. It's all-knowing. Invite more of it in, and let it melt all resistance. Notice as you do this that the light feels so much like home. It brings total comfort, safety, and support. Once you reach this point, you don't have to do anything to make the shift happen except be present and receptive. Divine intelligence takes over when you surrender.

Once you have formulated your intentions, be open and receptive. Allow yourself to receive with no resistance. Repeat these words to yourself:

I am willing to surrender and release all attachment, desire, and struggle.

I invite the light of the soul to fill me.

I am fully in the peace and comfort of the light.

I am willing to surrender and release the need for pain and suffering.

I surrender and release all aspects of ego and separation.

I surrender all needs of the ego.

I surrender myself to this process.

I give my full permission for this process to take place now.

The heart center is the doorway to your divine nature, and the solar plexus region is a gateway to the ego because it's where you hold attachments and the need to control your life. If you feel a tightening in the abdomen, it may be because of fear-based resistance to letting go. Just stay with the process, and keep repeating your intentions.

You may be surprised to know that each of your ego's subpersonalities has a voice that you can talk to. It's sometimes helpful to address the voices so you can understand them, which allows you to release them. The voices reflect the perceptions of the ego-identities and speak with all the authority of the ego.

Ask your subpersonalities to tell you what they believe and what they want. Ask them why they are there and whether they would like to be healed. Talk with them much the way you would with a person you want to get to know and understand. Don't expect everything they say to make sense; often it won't, but it will give you insights into the views the ego holds and why it's holding them, including insight into the ego's core fears.

As you surrender your fear, allow the subpersonality to melt from your awareness, since it isn't real. Feel into the depth of the subpersonality. Be aware of it. Feel it. Just observe and allow the sensations to float to the surface and dissolve into the light. You might even notice that, as more of the ego dissolves, the voice and objections of the subpersonalities become more fragmented and make even less sense. Just let it happen.

Now say the following words:

I am willing to surrender and release all resistance.

I surrender and release everything that's not the pure light of my soul.

I surrender and release everything that's of the ego.

I surrender and release the need for the ego's fears.

I call upon the hierarchy of all the angels, and I ask for their help.

I give the angels of healing permission to clear, heal, and support me.

Let yourself feel the extra help. Feel supported in allowing the clearing and healing to happen. Sense and allow the angels to support and help you.

Keep surrendering into the process. The light of spirit goes wherever you are. It's always with you. You might have intellectually known this in the past, but you may not have fully realized it. Now you can move into the realization of this truth.

Allow the deep grip of the pain and struggles to release as the whole premise of separation dissolves. Allow yourself to move into any feelings of being hopeless, cutoff, and abandoned, and bring the light and soul presence with you.

Let the sensations and realizations of the light, which is the Source energy, God energy, all intelligence, and all love, move into all the places where you were grasping and attaching. Invite it in to surround you, and feel its embrace.

The light was always there all the time, but you may have lived as though it weren't there and didn't exist. You don't have to try to make the light do anything. Just invite it in; it knows precisely where to go, what to do, and how to do it. It's like the sun shining inside you; that sun is your soul. This is who you truly are.

Give the light permission to integrate into all areas of your life. You want this light to flow into your work, into your relationships, and into everything that you say, think, and do. This process puts you into a state of mindfulness all the time, and dissolves anything that keeps you from being mindful, so it's effortless and automatic. This is your truth. Acknowledge and know that once this process starts, it will continue until it arrives at completion. Express gratitude for what you've received.

Now bring yourself back to your normal waking consciousness, feeling the new freedom you've gained. Keep inviting the process to continue, and surrender to the process a little more each day.

Chapter 8

the DEATH *of* FEAR

You're actually changing your history
by moving all of your experiences
to a higher reality.

Discovering the nature of a problem is 90 percent of resolving it. As you explore the subtleties of your issues and patterns, the process of discovery may take you deeper than you might at first have expected. This is because all problems have roots deep within the core structure of the ego, and the ego makes such a complete claim on our identity that sometimes removing an issue or pattern can seem as complex and daunting a task as removing color set in fabric.

All the traits of the ego operate in the foreground as well as in the background of our personality. These traits influence who we think we are, and their characteristics often take over and control us before we realize what's happening. If we attempt to eliminate problems caused by the ego by attacking them directly with various techniques, often we succeed only in removing a symptom, and another symptom pops up to take its place. Treating only the symptom is like pulling the top off a weed but leaving the roots. As any gardener knows, the weed will grow back. Only by pulling out the root of the problem we will eliminate all other permutations of it.

This chapter contains two very thorough meditations that will help you remove the roots of all fear and deepen the soul presence. But first we will focus more closely on the first stage of the soul-solution clearing process, identifying the problem. In this chapter, we'll address the fundamental core of the ego's fear. This is important because, as we've seen, fear is the basis of all the ego's defense mechanisms. Again, this is different from the kind of fear that activates when you're physically threatened. If a big dog lunges at you growling and barking, you'll quite naturally feel fear. This kind of fear reaction is wired into the brain and nervous system as a survival mechanism, and it energizes us for either fight or flight.

As you've seen, however, the kind of everyday fears most people feel are more often insecurities, self-judgments, doubt, guilt, second-guessing, worry, and anxiety. Such things as fear of rejection, fear of making a mistake, fear of not being liked, and many other fears make us feel cautious, self-conscious, vulnerable, and isolated, not more safe.

GETTING AT ROOT CAUSES

The first phase of the soul-solution clearing process is to identify the nature of your fear. You must tune in deeply and get an awareness of the complexity of the fear issue. This doesn't necessarily mean analyzing the intellectual details, but rather means sensing the subtleties that compose it, by exploring feelings, beliefs, conclusions, opinions, the need for control, repulsions, wants, and desires. As we've discussed, in the discovery phase you need to be a kind of detective.

The Story of the Ego's Birth

Along with the very personal parts of your own complex fear patterns, there are larger, more universal underpinnings. Let's consider once again how you got where you are in the big-picture sense. Remember, everyone started existence in a state of complete oneness in the light. From the beginning you experienced total and complete unconditional love, nurturing, acceptance, happiness, fulfillment, and connection with all there is. From this state, you curiously wondered what separation would be like, and before you realized what was happening, you were pulled into the experience of separation from the light and were quickly engulfed by a void of separation. What actually happened is that the very thought of separation created the separation.

The ego concluded you must have done something horrible to get in this situation, which generated feelings of fear and self-condemnation, and this subsequently formed a blueprint that regulated all of your lifetimes afterward.

What you did from this point on is unique to you. People make slightly different choices and decisions about how to cope, but there are similarities. The bottom line is, as you attempted to resolve the isolation and fear, a desperation arose within you — or, more precisely, within your ego — to survive at all costs.

Illusion and the Ego's Tool of Attachment

The ego doesn't know what's wrong or what's missing; it just knows that *something* is, so it tries attaching to everything it can in an effort to attain completeness and the feeling of being stable, safe, and secure. Attachment is the ego's primary tool. It can be attachment to people, places, things, knowledge, ideas, feelings, power, beliefs, control, possessions, fame, or an addiction. In fact, the entire physical universe serves the ego's need for attachment. The physical realm is of the ego, by the ego, and for the ego.

The process is much like when people are drowning and grab onto anything, including others in the water with them, even if it means pulling those people down, too, so that they both drown together. The ego starts grabbing onto whatever's nearby in order not to feel so lost, alone, insecure, and cut off, thinking that what it's attaching to is a kind of life preserver.

The ego exists inside walls of its own creation, but the answer to what it hungers for lies outside those self-created walls of separation from the light and the divine. The ego exists in a finite universe, but the answers aren't to be found there. The amazing paradox is that the walls don't even exist. They're illusions, but the ego believes in them so strongly that they present a convincingly real universe of separation. The walls of separation never existed, but like objects in a dream, they seem very real. When you're in a dream, all the characters and objects in the dream seem real, but when you wake up, the dream is revealed to be an illusion and its substance vanishes.

Again, what happened is that when the initial shock of separation occurred, fear caused you to encapsulate yourself in a dark shell. You closed your awareness to the light. You never actually left the light, and you didn't really move from one place to another. You didn't move into a real void because the void was and is an illusion. You created the appearance of a void with the belief that you separated from light and the soul, but the thought of separation was a complete illusion projected by the mind thinking and imagining what it believed happened.

However, from the moment you first imagined the possibility of separation, you became so completely absorbed in your own illusions of separation that you proceeded to live out many lifetimes as if those fearful illusions were real. You've been punishing yourself all those lifetimes for something that never even happened!

Another useful analogy is that of watching a movie. When you're in the theater, you become so absorbed in the drama that you respond as if the movie were real. You feel as if you know the characters, and you experience their emotions, but when you leave the theater, you walk back into your own world. You recognize the movie is a fiction even though for a little while it felt real. We tend to believe that feeling something is evidence of its being real. The fact that we have a feeling may be true, but what the feeling is based on is a creation of the mind. Similarly, the pain, suffering, struggle, joy, and happiness you experience in your life certainly feel real. Yet they're no more real than the fictional experiences of a movie character. Your mind creates all of it.

ACKNOWLEDGING AND DISIDENTIFYING

Understanding how you got where you are through the ego's defense strategies prepares you for the second step in the soul-solution process of clearing and releasing ego-based fear. This second step requires acknowledging what you've learned from the first step — the results of your detective work into the root causes of your fear — and being still in that awareness.

It's important to acknowledge that the problem, issue, or pattern isn't the real you. This entails the simple but crucial process of acknowledging and disidentifying: You connect with the issue and declare that you are not the issue and the issue is not you. You may actually be experiencing a pattern created long ago, or even one that may have been an inherited trait. In any case, it's not the real you. It's only like a recording or a movie playing in your mind. So you affirm, "I am not this. I do not own this, and I do not allow it to own me because I recognize my only true reality is my soul and divine essence."

HEALING THROUGH THE UNIVERSAL LOVE OF YOUR SOUL

After you've completed the step of acknowledging and disidentifying, the third step of the soul-solution process of clearing fear involves allowing the universal love of your soul to emerge in your consciousness and shift your awareness toward receiving progressively greater capacities of love and light, which will automatically and naturally dissolve the problem, issue, or pattern and remove the fear.

The meditations in this chapter give you an in-depth experience of this process. While there's a great deal of information to absorb in the meditations, the most important thing is to let yourself follow the narrative and have the experience. Allow your focus to be on the *experience* rather than on the words, which are only necessary to help give you a framework for understanding.

If you allow this experience to fill your consciousness, you're on the path to the elimination of ego-based fear once and for all.

MEDITATION

Releasing Fear at Its Source

Allow yourself to get comfortable, relaxed, and centered in your usual way.

Settle in, and hold the intention that in this meditation

you'll be releasing fear at its source. Just relax and follow the words. For the first part of this meditative process, simply follow the story.

When you originally separated from Source and were suspended in isolation, you felt a very deep sense of abandonment. Using your imagination, you can project yourself to this place now and recall some of what that experience was because you have been there and experienced it. The moment is actually in your memory because you've been living in this separation ever since. This condition defines human existence until enlightenment occurs. Since the separation occurred in a nonphysical universe without time, you can reconnect with it as if you were recalling a memory or even re-experiencing it now. It might feel a little like floating in the emptiness and darkness of outer space.

Now you can connect with the point of separation by looking inside of yourself for feelings of aloneness, abandonment, helplessness, and fear. These are feelings common to all of us because we've all gone through a similar experience before we were in human form and even before the physical dimension existed.

Your intention and your consciousness are your tuning devices to take you back to that event and the subsequent aloneness and emptiness that emanated from the experience of feeling separated. All feelings of aloneness, abandonment, helplessness, and fear originated here.

Hold the intention of going all the way back to the beginning of your existence in separation. As you do, notice an all-encompassing feeling of being isolated, so that no matter which direction you turned, you perceived only darkness. You heard nothing. You saw nothing. All you had was yourself and your own thoughts and consciousness.

The first feelings you became aware of were abandonment, isolation, and aloneness. The thought went through your mind, "Oh no, where am I?" This state of existence sharply contrasts with the original state of unity in which you lived in a total immersion of unconditional love. You were supported, nurtured, and nourished in love. Then everything became black, cold, and cut off, and nothingness was all around you. Notice that your reactions had an element of horror and terror.

Be aware of these feelings as a detached observer, as if you were watching a movie. It's okay; you're perfectly safe to do this. Your soul is traveling through this process with you. Observe the next thing that comes out of this place.

This is the origin of the core fear that started at separation, and since that time, fear has found ways to gain control through many, many lifetimes. Fear leads you to form false conclusions about yourself, such as feeling that something is wrong with you or you're not good enough. You conclude that you wouldn't be feeling so isolated and fearful if you were good enough. You deduce that obviously something must be wrong or even bad about you; otherwise, you'd still be in unity, love, and light.

Now the second step in this process is to recognize that the fear — the aloneness, abandonment, and helplessness — isn't you. It isn't your soul or true self. It's an aspect of consciousness that has lived in separation and therefore doesn't even know what trust is, or what the soul and light are, so it experiences fear.

Light and your soul are actually in you and all around you, but as you fear and resist life, you tighten and squeeze the opening to that awareness until it's so small that you're barely aware of it. Light and your soul still exist the same as they always have, but you've reduced the amount of the light and soul presence that can reach you at a conscious level.

While you're recognizing fear, also recognize and acknowledge once again that it's not you. Explore its cause: Fear originated from being cut off from your soul. I'm speaking of the core fear that started when you first experienced separation and ever since then has been finding ways to gain control through many lifetimes.

To find your way out of the illusion, all you need to do is remember the love and light and bring them back into your awareness. It's a little like opening your closed eyes to see the light in a well-lit room. Look up and look around, and see that light is there. It may seem a long way off because you've lived so many lifetimes away from it, but it's completely present in you, around you, and through you. Your soul has never left the light. The ego has been suffering under the illusion of separation and has been convincing you that it's real. Invite the light and divine presence in, and surrender to it.

Now, recall a familiar awareness and a clear memory that has been with you for eternity. This is the remembrance of a time when you lived in the light. I want you to go back to that moment just before you moved into the separation and fear. Put your awareness on the light in you and all around you.

Say to yourself:

I feel the light.

As you put your awareness on the light, experience an inner shift in your awareness and realize you never really separated.

This is the key to being released from the ego's hold and from the ego's fear: You never really left the light and divine presence. Say the following words to yourself and make them your own:

I receive the light of my soul.

The soul's divine light is in me and around me.

I give myself permission to merge completely into the divine light of my soul.

As you begin to become aware of the truth and light, the ego-created illusions are absorbed into it. Surrender the fear, aloneness, and self-condemning judgments. At first, you may be aware of the ego's resistance and feel tempted to stop the process. You may feel fear or think God will never accept you. You may hear a voice telling you that you're doing the wrong thing or that this will never work.

As you embrace more of the light, the ego's voices and feelings begin to fade and the objections diminish until they completely dissolve. Stay with the light. Stay with the soul.

The ego's experience consists of events it creates for itself. The separation was an illusion born out of a desire for that experience, and it intensified with time. In actuality, separation from God is impossible. Yet every experience in every lifetime has been lived as if it were real. Within your soul is love, light, and consciousness, which is who you truly are.

The first part of becoming the totality of who you truly are is to recognize that the fear in and around you isn't you. Fear is an experience stored in the ego. The fear is that if you let go of the fear, you'll cease to exist, resulting in annihilation. This is the core ego fear that keeps the ego clutching and holding on. This is what drives you to grasp and attach to things. It's why the ego is always driving you to want more. The ego is afraid that if it stops acquiring and holding on, it will die and cease to exist.

Acknowledge that you are not the fear, and say:

I am willing to completely surrender and release the need for fear.

I am willing to completely surrender and release helplessness.

I surrender everything that I am not.

I surrender all illusions.

If any voices of resistance arise, just say, "I surrender all need for them," and repeat back the voice of the resistance. The surrendering allows space for the light to enter and dissolve it. You can't make this process happen. Give it space and permission to happen. This is a natural progression of remembering rather than of doing.

It is my intent and my desire to fully reconnect with the light and universal love.

I invite the light into all parts of me that feel threatened and helpless or have difficulty trusting this process.

I surrender completely into the full awareness of love and light.

I surrender myself more and more deeply.

I surrender more and more deeply to love.

The light is love, and the light is God.

I remember the light.

I remember the love.

I give myself permission to deeply embrace the light and love.

Feel the process, and allow the light to move into the places that have felt threatened. This includes any part of you that wants to hold on to anything, such as beliefs, ideas, possessions, people, and feelings of pain, loss, or lack. Surrender attachments to them all.

Attachment is the ego's desperate attempt to prevent its annihilation. The ego tries to attach to everything because it's so terrified that it will be destroyed. This is why the illusions are so strong and keep perpetuating themselves. Because the ego is fighting for its very survival, it shrouds each lifetime with the darkness of illusion.

Open, and allow the energy of creation and the purity of love and light to flow into all your resistance and tightness. Recognize they're only illusions claiming you. They only seem strong because you've given them the energy that makes them appear real, but they have no reality. Say to yourself:

I give myself permission to deeply embrace light and love.

If you feel a density or fear, invite the light of your soul to merge into it. This melts the resistance as you keep inviting in more and more of the light presence. Let the light fill every atom and every space between atoms in your entire being.

Keep giving yourself permission to bring in the light of the soul, and know that the light is pure intelligence and pure love.

Say the following words to yourself and make them your own:

I allow myself to lift into the light.

The divine light is my truth — it's who I am.

I allow the light of my soul to expand through me.

Let the soul and light flow into all parts that aren't trusting or are questioning, and into all parts that feel helpless.

The light feels good.

I feel safe, secure, and comforted in the presence of the soul.

Invite the soul and light into any tightness built of fear.

I allow myself to receive more and more light.

You may perceive it as white light, as transparent white light, or as soft golden light. Surrender to the experience.

I allow the light of my soul to permeate me and saturate me with its presence.

Invite the soul and light into the parts of you that think or feel that you aren't good enough or that something's wrong with you.

I feel taken care of by the presence of my soul.

I know I am taken care of by the presence of my soul.

Allow the light to radiate and heal all separated parts. The light permeates all. Sense light radiating all around you.

I feel filled with the light.

I feel the presence of my soul.

Invite the soul and light into all the parts that hold on to any beliefs, ideas, people, or possessions.

I bathe and saturate in my soul and in the pure light and presence.

Invite the resistance to express itself. Get in touch with any of the words, objections, or resistance. Just listen. Do not dialogue. Just observe the resistance, and invite it to be present.

As you hold your attention on it, the resistance will dissolve in the light. Invite the light to engulf the resistance. Allow the soul and light to move into all the parts that hold on.

Once you give the soul and light permission to come in, they do. This is a natural process. Surrender to the light. Invite it in, and give it space to come in because it will flow in naturally and automatically. You don't have to make it do anything. All you have to do is allow it. The soul and light are naturally there, but the structures of resistance have held them out. The light totally surrounds and engulfs you and all resistance.

Know that you live in the light. You are the light. Sense the light radiating from within to fill all of your mind, body, thoughts, and feelings.

Take a deep breath now, and as you exhale give thanks

for what you've experienced during this meditation. Then slowly bring yourself back to your normal waking consciousness.

FEAR CANNOT EXIST
UNLESS WE FEED IT ENERGY

Part of what the Releasing Fear at Its Source meditation helps you experience is that resistance isn't real. The mind will hold it, but when the will is withdrawn, the resistance has no energy to sustain it. While it exists, it's like a monster from a nightmare arising from your subconscious that draws on your life-force energy to sustain itself, but once you identify the specific nature of the resistance and recall your life-force energy — withholding energy from it by becoming a detached observer — it runs down like an old windup clock.

When you become neutral, nonjudgmental, and nonreactive, you eliminate contributing energy that sustains the resistance or reaction. Then it runs down like a spent battery. It can put up resistance for a while, but sooner or later the resistance, like the battery, will run out of energy and stop. So the resistance really can't mount a sustained fight. It lacks the resources. The little energy it does have is infinitesimal compared to the soul's. As the light engulfs it, the resistance melts and disappears like the wicked witch in the film version of *The Wizard of Oz*, who said "I'm melting" after she was splashed with water. The truth of who you are is the light, and the light won't hurt anything that has a real existence. Everything else is an illusion. The next meditation shows how you can banish fear forever by embracing the light of the soul.

Embracing the Light of the Soul

To download a free recording of the author reading this meditation, use the code "SoulFilledHeart" at www.JonathanParker.com.

Once again allow yourself to get comfortable, relaxed, and centered in your usual way.

Arrange yourself until you are comfortable. Settle in, and hold the intention to enter meditation.

Invite the soul and light into any parts or places that are hurting, holding, or suffering. Let the soul and light flow to those places. Request that the soul and light merge into all thoughts, beliefs, memories, and feelings associated with the issues or patterns calling for your attention.

Repeat these thoughts in your mind and make them your own:

I request and receive more and more light.

I invite the divine light of my soul to fill me and surround me.

I receive the divine light presence of my soul deeply into me.

Surrender, release, and give yourself permission to allow in the light and presence of the soul. Don't even wonder if you're doing it right. Just allow yourself to receive the transformational presence in response to your requests.

I allow the soul light presence to saturate through me.

I am open and receptive to bringing the soul light into every part of my being.

Hold a relaxed state of surrendering to the process, and invite the light of the soul in more and more.

I feel at home in the light presence of my soul.

I feel the radiance of the soul light within me.

Every structure, every subtle body, every perception, every belief, and all the parts of your mind are projections from the state of separation, and since the soul's light and presence are very intelligent, the soul knows how to move through every layer and every frequency and clear the illusions. It is a saturating presence, so be like a sponge and absorb it, letting it into every cell of your mental body, your emotional body, and all your subtle bodies.

I feel suspended in an ocean of the divine light presence of my soul.

Let every cell soak in the light and be saturated by it. The light of the soul is love — like a pure, liquid essence of love with vibrant intelligence, and it radiates and permeates you at every level.

If any doubts come to your mind, such as "Am I doing this right?" "I don't know if it's happening," or "I don't know if I can do this," just surrender those thoughts and let the light presence of the soul dissolve them. Keep surrendering to the process.

Begin to notice that any voices of resistance are like voices in the wilderness. They are empty and unable to attach to anything. They are just leftover structures without foundations, and they're dissolving at this very moment.

Notice that although you may hear the voices, they're just empty voices composed of words, but the energy behind the words is gone, and you're just hearing leftover fragments of patterns.

Reinforce this process of release by using the following effective energy-clearing technique: Ask the energy of your core fear to turn a color, and then hold the intention of releasing all of that color. You can help the process along by asking all parts of you that don't know if you can do this, and therefore are in fear, terror, and illusion, to turn dark blue.

Make an inner request, and hold the intention for the fear you've identified to turn dark blue. Now notice all the dark blue energy in and around you, and release it all. You can imagine it dissolving or releasing into the earth, where it's neutralized and disappears — effectively uncreating into nothingness. Release everything that is not your soul in any dimension, in any frequency. Notice it releasing and dissolving. Release all barriers to the final return to oneness.

The truth cannot be threatened. Any fears that arise are not truth. Only the illusions are threatened. Be aware of any questions or concerns that come up as the soul presence moves into the parts of your awareness that are owned by the ego. As questions arise, observe them dissolve. No pushing, pulling, trying, or doing is necessary. Surrender further to the light.

Repeat these thoughts in your mind and make them your own:

I give myself permission to merge completely into the pure, divine essence of my soul.

I allow the presence of my soul to expand all through me.

I love the light and presence of my soul.

I feel grateful for the presence of the divine light in me.

As you become clearer, surrendering into and merging with the light, the light and the soul appear with a more refined and brilliant quality, and you're in touch with more levels of deep love, deep peace, and deep satisfaction. The more you invite them in, the more joy, bliss, and fulfillment you feel, and the more these qualities take over your whole being. This is an ever-increasing and ever-expanding experience that never ends. Allow yourself to remember how good reconnecting with the soul and the light feels.

The presence of my soul is comforting and healing.
I feel the presence of my soul.

Give the soul and light permission to integrate into all areas of your body, your mind, your life, your work, your relationships, and all your interactions with others.

I saturate myself in the light of my soul.

This experience is now with you always, no matter what you're doing. Even when you're distracted by daily duties, it's still operating, and you'll still notice its presence.

Give thanks for what you've experienced during this meditation, and slowly bring yourself back to waking consciousness. Bring your awareness fully into your body and into the room where you're doing this meditation, with the fullness of all realizations, vibrations, light, essence, consciousness, awareness, and experiences fully integrating all through you.

A PARADIGM SHIFT

Engaging in the soul-solution process to clear fear effects a paradigm shift. Over time, as a result of practicing the two meditations in this chapter, you'll notice a difference in both the way you respond to other people and the way they respond to you.

Keep going deeper and deeper into the experience, since the soul and light are infinite. As you go progressively deeper and continue with your practice of the meditations, the quality of the experience changes. Each time you absorb more light and presence, the ego dissolves more fully and therefore doesn't filter experiences as much as before.

This enables you to let in more love and more light each time you do this type of meditation. The realizations deepen as you gain access to new levels of awareness. You're getting in touch with your true self. This is your soul. Pain, fear, or any other negative experience that you've identified with are not you. The ego created all of them in the state of separation, and they have no real existence. As you've seen, the entire movement through the universe of separation was an illusion created by a belief in separation that wasn't real.

Since the ego isn't real, it actually isn't very strong, even though it may seem to have a great deal of power over your life right now. But in truth, the ego possesses a very weak energy field because it's a total illusion, and therefore it cannot resist the light or sustain itself within the presence of the soul.

Living in and identifying with separation and fear is like pulling the covers over your head in the morning to block out the light so that you can continue sleeping. Similarly, when you pull the covers of separation over you, it only prevents you from seeing the light that's there. All you have to do is pull the covers back down to see that the light was there all the time. Bringing the light into the darkness dispels it, enabling you to live as an individual and at one in the light and in the soul's presence.

The two meditations in this chapter offer a powerful way to do clearing and healing because they take you back to the very source of all pain, struggle, and disease. At this place in consciousness, you recognize that all of these are illusions and that fear results from your decision to live in darkness instead of light. When you go back to the moment when that choice was made, you can choose the light and embrace it to re-create your history. You're actually changing your history by moving all of your experiences to a higher reality as you embrace the light of your soul.

Part Three

the SOUL-SOLUTION GUIDE
to HEALING and ENLIGHTENMENT

Knowledge opens a door,
but you must enter by yourself.

— CHINESE PROVERB

Chapter 9

WHAT DOES YOUR SOUL WANT?

*Each condition or event that comes to you
is your soul's guidance as it moves you forward. Each step
advances you closer to home.*

Part 2 introduced you to the basic principles of the soul-solution process and offered meditations guiding you in how to dissolve the original separation and fear of the ego. Part 3 looks more specifically at how these principles can help you release the pain of your personal past and allow you to heal anything in your life that's troubling you.

HOW THE PAIN OF THE PAST THREATENS US

People set themselves up for difficulties through their memories of pain. For instance, in the past, you or someone you know may have lost money, a job, a house, or a relationship. These issues, rife with fear and other negative emotions, establish a deep pattern in memory and the subconscious. Then, when you hear something on the news or when someone you know tells you a similar story, the pattern triggers the memory, reminding you of the past pain and struggles. At such times, inner voices are activated, saying things like, "Remember when you suffered something similar? Well, watch out. It could happen again! It could be coming your way right now, so be very careful!"

In this way, people tend to use their own history to validate an imagined threat even when a real threat doesn't exist. Ironically, by imagining the possibility of a threatening situation, people set themselves up to manifest it, since the nature of the mirror universe reflects back whatever we hold in consciousness.

HOW YOUR PAST BECOMES YOUR FUTURE

The truth is, many people live as if their past isn't really past. They live as though everything from the past is a reality right now. Even if people believe that something happened to them in a past life, they often live as if the pattern is still real now. It's as if they're hypnotizing themselves into believing that the issues of the past are real today. As a result, they internalize the related patterns, and the conditions they feared eventually become real.

In every life, forces from the past create obstacles. If you look back on your own life, you'll see that some of your experiences hit you where you felt the most vulnerable. If you've noticed this, you're not alone, because it happens to almost everyone.

You may have heard the saying, "The mills of the gods grind slowly, but they grind exceedingly fine." As a child I never understood what this saying meant, but as I grew older, I began to understand that we all face the mill of experience that grinds and forms our character traits. We then resist the experiences, refine them, or release them. If we resist, the mills keep grinding. The grinding stops when we discover the way to let go of the resistance. At that point, we experience relief and find more ease and flow.

The mind and ego continually create false reasons to justify lack, struggle, and suffering, and since these reasons stem from faulty assumptions, perceptions, and conclusions, if we want our releasing techniques to be effective, they need to address these fabrications. Certainly retaining the wisdom of the past without holding on to the suffering from the emotional pain is useful. But to do this, we must be willing to surrender and release the pain and suffering connected to the patterns the mind has created.

The first step in releasing anything is to identify some details about what you're releasing. This may seem obvious, but the process entails more than meets the eye. To begin with, you need to spend a little time exploring the nature of the discomfort and its causes. Once again, this is the first phase of the soul-solution process: You have to be a bit of a detective to learn what the discomfort is all about. This will pay off with rich rewards when it comes to releasing and letting go. You don't have to go deeply into the feelings you uncover in the process, but engage them to the extent that you can describe them. The more you identify and describe them, the more you'll release. And the more you release and let go of the grip of suffering and struggle, the more you'll be able to experience the natural goodness and happiness of your soul.

Once you've identified the suffering and struggling, you progress to the second phase in the soul-solution process, acknowledging what you've uncovered in the first step. You then willingly disidentify with the position while affirmatively stating that you're letting it go. Here are some examples of the kinds of statements you might make at this stage: "I am willing to surrender and release the need for fear and anxiety. I am willing to surrender and release the need for loss and lack. I am willing to surrender and release the need for struggling."

Of course, your own releasing statements can be far more

specific and detailed; use this wording as a guideline. Besides describing the issue, it's important to engage your emotions, since that's what energizes the releasing statements. While these statements seem simple enough, they'll be far more effective if you also connect with the underlying feelings.

Put another way, if you do this process merely as a mental or intellectual exercise, the results will be limited, but if you truly connect with and feel the words, you'll experience the desired relief. And if you also include bringing in the soul presence — the third step of the soul-solution process — you can become completely free.

SEVEN STEPS TO TAKE
WHEN YOU'RE STUCK WITH AN ISSUE

Now let's get more detailed about how you can deal with challenges, blocks, or reactions you experience stemming from troubling issues or patterns in your life. You can apply these seven steps to any deep-seated core pattern you face, including issues related to the pain of the past.

Here are the steps:

1. Acknowledge your reaction.
2. Determine the purpose of the issue.
3. Ask yourself what your soul wants you to grow into.
4. Send your soul and deep love to your issue.
5. Be open to the truth behind what you're experiencing.
6. Bless everything in your world.
7. Surrender your burdens, and experience the light of the soul.

You'll notice that, in essence, these seven steps simply expand on the three-step soul-solution process first described in chapter 5.

You'll be using variations on these steps in the meditations on healing throughout part 3, which will allow you to anchor them more fully in your consciousness.

To bring the seven steps into clear focus, keep in mind an issue of concern while you read. It could be something you feel trapped by or something that triggers a strong reaction. The issue could be physical or emotional, or it could be a person or an event that triggers the negative reaction. Take a moment to bring it to mind. When you have the issue clearly in mind, read through the following steps.

Step One: Acknowledge Your Reaction

The first step entails acknowledging your reaction and becoming a witness of yourself and your issue. You may have gone along for many years thinking that your life is a story with traps set along the way. You may think that you're cursed by karma or bad luck. But whatever your experience is, there's a process at work, and acknowledging it is important. A force moves through your life that you've likely felt but perhaps haven't understood. Your soul is working to unfold something from within, and it does this by pushing ego defense patterns to the surface.

Your inner guide and soul are always moving you to uncover your truth, but it takes sifting through layers of struggle or pain. Layers rise to the surface for you to examine. At such times it's easy to view others as responsible for your issue, but such a view is usually distorted. Step one calls for clarity and asks you to see the issue as it really is.

In this first step, you merely recognize and acknowledge the issue and the people involved. The more you practice this process, the better you'll get at it. During this stage, it helps to extend mercy and compassion to yourself, and to be gentle and simply observe yourself.

As part of your healing work at this stage, spend some time just being with your reactions, whatever they are — anger, blame, fear, depression, judgment, or something else. Examine the descriptions, beliefs, and conclusions you associate with the issue, which may be a pattern that has had you caught for five or ten years or even more. Also go further and identify your reactions: What do you do with them? How do you experience them? How do they affect you?

Remember that your reactions and responses are all signals that your soul is bringing to the surface something that needs to be addressed. Your soul puts issues and circumstances in front of you until you address and clear them, and your soul will do this repeatedly. It's up to you to choose what to do with the situation and your reactions. If you ignore your reactions or go into denial, they'll submerge and reappear again and again until you clear them. This is why most people have patterns that seem to keep repeating. Your task is to explore your positions and reactions and identify them in some detail in order to fully release them.

Step Two: Determine the Purpose of the Issue

The second step involves asking yourself: "What is this pattern for? What is it leading to? What has it been trying to do? What is it trying to create? What is its goal?" During this step, ask yourself how you would describe your positions and reactions in greater depth. You might want to imagine that you're explaining your answers to these questions to a trusted friend.

Step Three: Ask Yourself What Your Soul Wants You to Grow Into

The third step entails acknowledging what your soul wants you to grow into. Ask yourself: "Do I want this issue in my life, or do I want the love and light of my soul?" This is your place of choice. The question may seem easy to answer, and it may seem obvious, but pinpointing your position and stating it to yourself are key. Instead of projecting the causes of conditions outside of yourself, you have the opportunity to make the choice to examine yourself. Ask yourself questions such as: "What's being presented to me?" and "What's important for me to see and understand?" Then state your answers to yourself. It's important to affirm your answer to this basic question: "Do I want this present condition, or do I want love and light?"

Once again, every situation is a mirror of some part of yourself. You may not believe something inside of you is reflected in the actions of others, but everyone and everything mirrors something inside of you. The difficulty with realizing this is that most of the patterns are below your conscious perception until you discover them, and then you find yourself saying, "Oh, now I see it." At that point, you may even wonder how you missed it before. During this third step, you acknowledge your reactions as a mirror of something inside of you.

Step Four: Send Your Soul and Deep Love to Your Issue

Your fourth step involves sending the soul and deep love to your issue. You'll want to do this very gently, easily, and softly. The method is simple: Breathe into your position and reactions, and then let go. Allow a sense of peacefulness to fill you as you tune in to the deep love and light of your soul, and ask your soul to merge into all of your feelings, positions, and reactions.

While engaging in the fourth step, it's important to hold the intention of maintaining an alignment with divine presence. The goal is to trust the wisdom of your own soul and send love and mercy to yourself. This will enable you to embody the divine light of your soul's presence. Keep opening these places inside of you deeper and deeper as you allow the light of your soul to come in, all the while relaxing and receiving the light of the soul's presence. This is also a good time to send blessings of love and light to any others involved.

As you clear and heal in this way, sometimes thoughts, feelings, and memories will come up. Whatever arises, your task is simply to keep opening, surrendering, and asking your soul to merge into it. Your soul and divine presence know what they're doing, so you can relax with the process. You don't have to know or do anything at this point other than to bring the soul and love presence into you with your intention of surrendering all resistance and opening to receive.

Be aware of how what's coming up affects you, and where the pain resides within. Then simply notice and be with it. In this way, you're bringing the light of divine presence and consciousness to the pain, with the intention that the presence of the clear light will fill you.

If you're tracking and following your thoughts, feelings, and memories, you'll be able to bring peace and love to them. You may or may not feel the effects immediately, but a response always occurs.

Your spiritual development enlarges your energetic heart space for all that's happening in the world. This will enable you to become more present with events, struggles, and suffering, meeting them with greater equanimity, love, and trust. In this way, you radiate your soul's qualities outward.

It's important to keep taking deep, relaxed breaths during this process, and to avoid holding or tightening. We are used to turning away from what hurts, and staying with your breath can help you be present.

Step Five: Be Open to the Truth behind What You're Experiencing

To explore more deeply the truth behind what you're experiencing, step five entails asking yourself more questions that go deeper than in the previous steps to reveal more layers of what is being experienced. In step five you can explore questions brought to the surface in step four, such as "What do I need to understand?" "What's the truth?" "What's the teaching?" "What's the wisdom?" "What's the lesson?" "What can I learn from this?" "What do I believe will happen if I let go of this?" "What will my life be like without this issue and reaction?" and "I know that every event is leading me somewhere; where am I being led?"

After you've explored these questions, it's a good idea to conclude by saying: "My beloved divine presence and soul, help me to understand what's important for me to realize from this experience." Then let yourself open and receive the truth, receive the love, receive the light. They are gifts.

For this step, it's important to keep allowing more and more light and awareness to fill you as the realizations deepen. You're becoming a beacon of mercy, love, light, and truth. We each have different gifts to share. As the light moves through you, you emit unique qualities. These qualities from your heart and soul create change and help you manifest the life you want.

Through saying yes to gifts from your soul, you keep progressing on your path. You may not know all the details about your future, but trusting your soul will lead you to a higher life. Again, each condition or event that comes to you is your soul's guidance as it moves you forward. Each step advances you closer to home.

Step Six: Bless Everything in Your World

Your sixth step in this process is to bless everything in your world that has assisted or resisted you each day. *Blessing* in this context simply means holding the intention for goodness, abundance, health, happiness, and love. When you bless everyone and everything in your life, you're recognizing that they've appeared because you've had some need for them.

Love is the way. With love, nothing seems difficult and nothing feels like a struggle. Everything becomes an opportunity to send forth more love and blessings.

As you engage in this act of blessing, it's a good idea to include all the people and situations that have caused you difficulty, including people you may resent or dislike, whether they're people from your past or your present. As part of this step, allow yourself to bless all of them with peace and goodness, happiness and prosperity, and wishes for their health. Your sincerity in this step makes all the difference.

Step Seven: Surrender Your Burdens, and Experience the Light of the Soul

The seventh step brings us to the all-important theme of surrender. *Surrender*, as I'm using the word, doesn't mean giving up. It isn't about loss, defeat, or resignation. It doesn't necessarily even require you to stop what you're doing. It simply means letting go, in every possible way, of pain, struggle, and resistance. Ultimately, it means the complete and total letting go of all forms of resistance and all attachments to everything. This doesn't mean you have to eliminate people or things from your life and live in isolation or renunciation. It only means that you're letting go of your attachments and judgments about it all.

This final step entails surrendering your burdens. Effective surrender comes from the heart, and from being in touch with or connecting with whatever you're surrendering. When we raise our consciousness and surrender and release our burdens, they transform into light and dissolve into nothingness. As your consciousness releases its final fears and doubts, all good manifests. More lifetimes are no longer necessary to achieve your enlightened destiny. It can be yours now.

As part of the seventh step, repeat these thoughts to yourself: "I am willing to release all need for the fear of releasing all fear. I am willing to release and let go of all resistance to resistance. I surrender and release all need for judgments."

Throughout your day, it's a good practice to say to yourself about everyone and everything: "May the divine presence within bless you!" The continued use of this statement will build a condition in which everything you're blessing blesses you in return, for this is the nature of the mirror universe.

As you conclude step seven, say to yourself: "I love you, my soul. I love the soul of everyone in my life. I love the soul of everyone. I love the soul of Mother Earth. I send blessings of goodness to all." When you repeat these statements, you'll notice the atmosphere surrounding you has a presence, a quietness, a richness, and a peacefulness. This is the essence of God's reality, which reveals itself through blessings and love. When you acknowledge that you live in an ocean of divine love and light, you attain a complete understanding of all there is. You can conclude the seventh step by saying to yourself: "I fully integrate all of these realizations into the fullness of who I am."

Chapter 10

HEALING *with* SOUL PRESENCE

As you discover who you are,
you also find the very traits you most aspire to.

In this chapter and the rest of part 3, we'll focus on applying the elements of the soul-solution process and the seven steps described in chapter 9 to bring healing to any area of your life that needs it.

You may have heard the story about the man who was looking for a lost key one dark night under a streetlamp. A friend passing by on the street stopped to ask him what he was doing, and then the friend got down on the ground to help him look. After searching for quite a while, the friend asked, "Are you quite sure you lost the key around here?"

"No, I'm not sure," the man replied. "I may have lost it inside."

The friend asked the obvious question: "Then why are you looking for it out here?"

"Because the light seems better here," the man replied.

In other words, people often look for answers in the wrong places. They look in what appear to be the easiest and most obvious places outside of themselves, but these seldom yield answers.

This story is a metaphor for people looking in the dark realms of the ego for answers that aren't there. All of our answers lie within.

An ancient spiritual tradition says that the problems we seek answers for are like the leaves and branches of a large tree. We can pull the leaves off and even cut off some of the branches, but the tree will keep growing more. The solution lies in chopping down and completely uprooting the tree. The tree is your ego. You can continue pruning the leaves and branches and finding ways of coping, but as long as the trunk and root system exist, it will continue sprouting forth with new ways to express itself.

YOU ALREADY ARE WHAT YOU'RE SEEKING

To discover who we are, and to find the solutions to our problems, we first need to look in the right place. So often we follow a convoluted path that leads us to various doctors, psychologists, and sociologists, who tell us how we — and our problems — are the products of biology, environment, culture, childhood, and life experiences. Some religions tell us that humans are weak, insignificant sinners whose problems are the natural result of our sinful state. The latter point of view no doubt derived from observing the many insecurities and instabilities of the ego.

All of these approaches keep people looking in the wrong places. They divert the search for our true nature into explorations of the realm of the mind and ego, all of which prevents most people from ever discovering their deeper self, or soul. The reason for the confusion is that the mind and ego, as we saw in part 2, simply cannot enter that realm.

Most people seem to believe that they're striving to *become* something. This would include creating and building desirable traits, characteristics, and qualities, such as *becoming* more kind, loving, noble, caring, insightful, generous, supportive, compassionate, wise, and all the other traits we admire in saints and spiritual leaders throughout history. But what we may not so readily understand is that those who possess these traits didn't *develop* them as such. They *revealed* these wonderful traits because they're the natural qualities of the soul.

When you discover your soul and come into relationship with it, its qualities automatically and naturally manifest in your life. So as you discover who you are, you also find the very traits you most aspire to. Your life changes, and the path that once challenged you is much smoother and easier to travel. This is the true secret behind all effective healing methods.

THE HIGHEST FORM OF HEALING

It has often been said that God is love. God, or Source, is the intelligent, unifying principle and force behind all things — the unifying energy we call love. Love is the essential energy that unites all form, structure, and imagination. When you connect with your soul and inner presence, you're connecting with an aspect of your divine Source that expresses itself through you. At such times, you're participating in your true nature. You're remembering your true self. You're recalling the essential energy and presence of love that your soul *is* by attuning your attention to the soul presence and inviting your soul and divine presence to enter your whole being.

With practice, this alignment with your soul leads your heart-soul consciousness to dissolve into the unifying principle of all things. You merge with the highest aspect of love and allow yourself to dissolve into it. Your spiritual work leads to immersion in love and divine presence through intention, surrender, and remembrance. It dissolves differences between your heart and the essence of divine love, thereby opening the way for you to experience all the beauty and essential qualities of your soul and divine presence, which is one way we could define *healing*.

As we discussed earlier, the spiritual heart center is the key to the soul-solution process, and the practice of attuning to the divine presence through it opens the heart to the soul and all its qualities, including deep love. This is the highest form of healing because it allows you to work directly with the soul and divine essence through the heart to bring yourself closer to your true nature and the unity of all creation. This completely dissolves the illusions of the ego, and at the same time it elevates you to a higher spiritual awareness. It can even bring about physical and emotional healing.

The first thing in any clearing or healing is determining what to work on. Sometimes you have a definite idea, and sometimes you're not sure, so it's always best to start with what's arising in your life at the present moment. In the next two meditations, I'll guide you through the soul-healing process, which you can use to heal physical, emotional, and mental disturbances, as well as to solve any problems you might be having with others. As with all the meditations in this book, these two meditations build on each other, and over time, as you practice them, you'll go deeper and deeper. This is especially true as you learn to heal your issues with the support of the soul presence.

MEDITATION

The Soul-Healing Process

Assume a comfortable and relaxed position, so you can go deeply inside and be in touch with the deepest parts of yourself.

Take a comfortable breath in through your nose, hold it for a moment, and then let it gently out through your mouth while you feel yourself relaxing. Let go of the outside world, so you can embrace your inside world.

Begin by tuning in to your inner space. Be open, and notice what has been stirring within you this day or recently. A mixture of things may be occurring in your life right now, but identify one issue or pattern in particular that you've recently been struggling with, confused about, in pain over, or uncomfortable with. It could be a specific issue you've been dealing with, or it could be a general feeling of being overwhelmed, insecure, fragile, frustrated, or discouraged.

Go inside yourself, and meet what's there. Just tune in to it, but don't be concerned about trying to change anything at this point. You're just gathering information now. Go inside, and acknowledge this place in you. Acknowledge and recognize its presence.

Are you in touch with your inner experience? If you're not comfortable with what you're finding, make space for not liking it or being uncomfortable with it. If you're not feeling anything, acknowledge this, because even not feeling anything is important information. You're simply observing yourself at this time.

Now settle your attention on the center of your chest. When I speak of your heart center in this healing context, I mean the entire area from your throat to your stomach. Drop your attention into your heart center and feel it. How does your heart-center space feel? Are the sensations there different from what you were noticing before?

Next, deepen your attunement with your soul and inner presence, and observe your experience. Put either hand over the center of your chest, and notice the subtle differences occurring within you. Some levels may be experiencing some disturbances, while others are manifesting great peace and expansion. Release all expectations of what you might discover. Some people may expect to experience transcendence and light, but instead may feel deep peace and beauty. You don't usually know in advance the fullness of what the experience will be, so just hold the intention to connect with — and be open to receive — your soul.

In attunement through the heart, you can merge into your soul and melt into divine presence. This process takes you through the doorways of consciousness to arrive at your deepest truth. Once there, you will find transformation of who you think you are. All of this transpires through letting go of all ego concepts or mental constructs you may have been holding on to. This is a surrender process that often leads to wonderful realizations.

Just pay attention to whatever is going on for you now. Notice your body and mind. Whatever you get in touch with, just breathe into it.

When you make space for what you're noticing, one of two things will likely happen. First, you may notice or feel your sensations more because you're open and accepting, and so what was below your conscious awareness before is now showing itself. If you're feeling some sensations even more strongly now than before you started this process, acknowledge them and allow all the revelations to continue.

On the other hand, a second possibility is that you might feel more peaceful and spacious. Either experience is possible, and both lead in a positive direction. As long as you stay in the moment and with what you're experiencing, there's nothing you can do wrong. Just acknowledge what's happening.

Next, put your attention on your heart center, and slowly repeat the phrase:

I feel my soul deeply in my heart.

As you say these words to yourself several times inwardly, call for the soul and divine presence to begin filling you while you continue the exploration. Do this for a few minutes before proceeding.

Now ask the soul and divine presence to merge into and clear whatever is presenting itself to you, and accept the process. Trust the process. Your soul knows exactly what you need, so just keep tracking your reactions and deepening into them.

Next, bring to your awareness a memory of one incident or story about the issue or pattern — ideally, one that epitomizes it. Be specific. If you want to clear or heal something, you need to know what you're clearing and healing. Remember the moment or day the incident happened, or when you discovered the condition or issue.

Call to the pure healing light of your soul and divine presence to merge into and radiate through the incident or story. Observe how your inner space is changing. Say to yourself:

I ask the highest awareness of my soul to merge into the sensations and thoughts around this issue.

I ask the light of the soul to radiate through this story or incident.

Observe anything that is taking place.

Now drop down a little deeper, and connect with the feelings associated with your story. As an observer, notice the quality of your feelings. Do they feel like an ache, like tightness, like pain, like sadness, or like some other sensation altogether? How do you describe your feelings to yourself? Are they dull, sharp, dense, heavy? What do they feel like?

After you have described the feelings associated with your story, inwardly call for the soul and divine presence to radiate through the feelings. Call to the pure healing light of the soul and divine presence to merge into and through the feelings. Say to yourself:

I ask the highest awareness of my soul to merge into these sensations and feelings around this issue.

I ask divine presence to radiate through these feelings.

Observe anything that takes place. Recognize that this issue has taken its toll. It has had an impact. Acknowledge to yourself that your judgments have affected you. What are your judgments about this condition?

See if you can identify any of the voices that emerge when you're in touch with this issue. Identify your self-talk, including self-judgments. What do you say to yourself about this issue?

Inwardly call for the soul and divine presence to merge into the voices and self-judgments, beliefs, and conclusions.

Call for the soul and divine presence to merge into the blame and self-blame. Call for the soul and divine presence to merge into the criticism and self-criticism.

Where in your body do you feel this quality? Where do you notice you've been carrying this in your body?

Now, as you breathe in, bring in light and your soul presence. Using the breath to carry your attention into all you're aware of is very important.

Receive the presence of your soul right to that spot. Breathe the soul right into the spot with your inner requests and intentions. There's no need to be forceful; there's actually little doing involved. The process engages through a gentle intention as you breathe into the spot. You may also notice a pure healing light or healing sensation coming into the spot.

Request that the light of the highest awareness of your soul merge into the issue with wave after wave of light, presence, and consciousness. Receive the softening, and allow the process. All you have to do is hold a clearing and healing space, and the soul's light and presence come in and manifest the clearing and healing.

Feel a deepening into the peace as you keep opening and receiving. Deepen into your heart, your soul, and your trust. Open yourself to receive deeper and deeper.

Opening yourself to receive opens a door that allows in the healing light. Open yourself to receive the healing light of your soul and divine presence.

As you continue with your attention on your heart area, keep inviting more and more soul and divine presence to emerge. As you do, you'll find that your capacity for receiving grows larger.

I ask my soul to radiate in me, through me, and around me.

Your heart space is a doorway that grows larger and larger. Continue opening to receive more love, light, and presence through your heart.

I feel my soul in my heart — deeper and deeper.

Repeat this phrase several times until you sense the peaceful presence around you. Then, when you feel ready to bring this meditation to a conclusion, take a deep breath and begin to shift your awareness to the place where you're meditating, and to being present in this moment. Feel your body in this new space.

Know that this soul-healing process will continue day and night long after this meditation is over, and allow it. You have requested and engaged a process that continues as long as necessary.

You have requested healing and transformation, so welcome and allow the transformations you've requested. Hold the intention of continuing to deepen into the healing process day and night. Enjoy the presence of these energies as you express gratitude for what you've received.

MEDITATION

Deepening the Soul-Healing Process

Begin your meditation by arranging yourself in a comfortable and relaxed position, in a place where you won't be disturbed.

Take a comfortable breath in through your nose, hold it for a moment, and then let it gently out through your mouth while feeling yourself relaxing. Take another deep breath in through your nose and hold it briefly, and then release it out through your mouth as if you are gently blowing out a candle, and feel yourself relaxing more deeply. Feel yourself releasing everything you're ready to release, especially any tension, holding, or stress.

Take another deep breath, hold it for just an instant, and then release it gently out through your mouth, and feel yourself releasing and letting go of any anxiety, uneasiness, or uncertainty.

Take another deep inhalation and exhalation, and feel yourself releasing and surrendering any questions or doubts.

Repeat these words to yourself:

I open to the fullness of the soul and divine light.

I allow the purity of the soul and divine light to fill me.

I allow the purity of the soul and divine presence to dissolve everything unlike itself within me.

Feel the soul and divine presence in your heart. Sense the natural, soft, nurturing, and healing presence it brings, and feel centered in your heart.

Now bring your consciousness to your breath. Simply begin to watch, observe, and feel the breath moving in and out. Observe the movement of your abdomen as it rises and falls with the breath. Just observe and continue feeling into the deepening presence of the love, light, and soul.

The breath opens doors for the soul's presence. Keep

watching the breath, and synchronize your intention to deepen into soul presence with your breath.

If you find any resistance to your peace, keep receiving the deepening presence of your soul, and direct the presence into the distraction wherever you notice it in your body, mind, or emotions. Say to yourself:

I call to the highest awareness of my soul to merge into my feelings.

Pain and struggle reflect energy patterns held in the unconscious. Release all attachments to the causes of the conditions, known or unknown, and deny that they have any reality. Often, unknown patterns are held in the unconscious. They are mere attachments you have collected over time that no longer serve you, and they are no more you than barnacles are the ship they cling to. They may go along for the ride, but that doesn't make them the ship.

Your reality and truth are your soul and your eternal self. Anything else is a counterfeit of truth presenting itself to you to be released. The ego will always let you know what's causing it pain and struggle through your feelings, conclusions, and judgments. These are the ego's way of waving a flag that says, "This is what's troubling me; please help me to release it."

Engaging the soul, and the process of surrendering, answers all questions and overcomes all pain and struggle. As your soul emerges more and more in your awareness, and merges into every illusion and frustration, it clears everything, purifying all as it deepens and returns everything back to its original innocence and completion.

Trust your heart in the embrace of your soul. Trust your heart in the embrace of divine light. Truly partake of the love and light, and let it overflow into your whole body. Surrender yourself deeper and deeper, and feel the presence bringing a soothing, nurturing, and healing peacefulness to your heart. Move into the stream of light and soul presence, and let it completely fill you and embody you. Keep opening your heart and going as deeply as you can.

What do you feel now that's different in your body as a result of this process? You might notice a lightness of being, a spaciousness and vastness, or clarity and brightness. You might sense that you're glowing, and feel awake and peaceful.

Feel the new energy, and remember it, because you want to evolve into feeling this way all the time. How would your life be if every cell in your body felt all the wonderfulness of the soul all the time?

Imagine tuning in to your body to experience the unlimited, infinite expansion of divine love and light through the core of your being. Every cell carries infinite love and beauty. Acknowledge a comforting river of love and divine presence flowing through every cell of your being from head to toe. As you do your meditation practices daily, you'll retain this moment and go even deeper.

Notice how things are becoming lighter. This is because you're moving away from the identity that held the pain. The identity that held the pain thins out and dissolves, allowing a peacefulness to come in naturally.

The light and presence of the soul come in when you

ask for them. When you tune in to them, they automatically dissolve issues. Clearing and healing allow for four possibilities: The issue can diminish in intensity; the issue can disappear completely; a disidentification from the issue can ensue so that there's less reaction to it as it moves farther away; or other pictures, memories, and feelings or more self-talk can emerge.

Because change comes in many stages, any of these four outcomes represents progress. Check in with yourself, and find out where you are on your journey with this issue. If any threads are incomplete, make note of them so that you can return to them at a later time.

Express gratitude for this process and the healing you've received, including the clearings that took place below your level of conscious awareness. Acknowledge to yourself:

I am blessed with love, beauty, and joy.

Now bring yourself back into your normal waking consciousness, and proceed with your day blessed by this process of healing.

Chapter 11

HEAL: HEALTH, ENLIGHTENMENT, ABUNDANCE, LOVE

*Healing is the process of allowing
your own creations to dissolve
and be replaced by a deeper truth.*

We can consider the word *heal* an acronym that defines the major aspects of what we want in life. HEAL stands for

Health
Enlightenment
Abundance
Love

The HEAL acronym summarizes all the areas where we would like to experience healing. Most people think of healing in relation to health, but healing applies in a broad sense to all four areas, each of which requires expanding your capacity to receive your soul and your true self.

Though this is seemingly self-evident, few approach healing this way. The most common approach is to use the force of our will and determination to accomplish the goals. This works to some degree in acquiring abundance, but it doesn't work very well in the remaining three areas. Some forms of abundance can certainly be acquired through diligent and determined effort, but enlightenment, love, and health by their nature don't respond well to force. Rather, they require surrender in order to be fully realized, and surrender is a receptive process, not an aggressive approach.

To accomplish our highest goals, we must be open to receiving them, which necessitates releasing all resistance around them. Areas not open to receiving your inner soul presence are those where you find struggle, suffering, confusion, and lack. All of these present blocks to fulfillment, and all of them are calling on you for release and clearing.

Sometimes people are afraid to receive because they fear they may then lose what they've gained, or perhaps they believe that they aren't worthy or deserving of something wonderful, or they think they weren't born with the skills or resources needed to obtain what they want. These reasons help explain why some people are fearful of receiving. Some fears are rooted in a negative self-image, which defeats people through feelings of inadequacy and a sense of not deserving the highest possible success and happiness. Other fears are rooted in a lack of confidence. In this case, people often don't even try because they're convinced they lack the skills and resources necessary for success.

THE KEY TO RECEIVING

Lack in any of the four arenas — health, enlightenment, abundance, and love — stems from resistance to receiving. Resistance is held through beliefs, perceptions, and projections, which are all forces that sustain the illusions of our world. We all have them. We develop them as we grow up and observe the experiences of ourselves and others. In most cases, however, we never consider that the source of lack may lie within.

Health, enlightenment, abundance, and love — or HEAL

— are all dependent upon inner rather than outer factors. This fact becomes apparent as you deepen your inner connection with your soul — the source of all fulfillment.

To begin this process, it's crucial to open the heart center, which is the gateway to clearing the blocks and resistance impeding your progress. Once these blocks are cleared, you'll easily receive the abundant blessings of the soul. In this respect, the heart center also serves as the most easily accessed portal to the soul and the deep, core essence of your being.

You can begin this process now by putting your attention on your soul center, in the center of your chest, and requesting to tune in to, connect with, and sense the presence of the *highest enlightened awareness of your soul* — a phrase I'll be repeating in the next few chapters. By making this request and holding this intention, you'll begin to open a door that has always been there. This is the door to your real self and a deeper reality than what you're normally aware of with your five senses. Your willingness to surrender and let go of any form of resistance opens the door.

A key to healing and arriving at where you want to be is allowing what you've created to be dissolved by the love and presence of your soul. Healing and clearing the path to an awakened and enlightened life is the art of learning to bring the presence of the soul into the struggle or the lack that covers the deep love and truth that's within. You accomplish this through a process of merging every aspect of who you think you are with your soul, in order to experience who you *really* are.

THE HEART OF THE MATTER

The heart center, or heart chakra, is the energy center in your body that most easily experiences life from the soul's point of view. The heart center includes a spiritual and an emotional aspect, and the spiritual heart center is always available, although you may not always feel it's open. This isn't because the *spiritual heart* is ever really closed, but because the *emotional heart* is. The emotional heart is an energy center surrounding your spiritual heart.

For example, for many people, trust issues often come up when opening the heart because they have had disappointing emotional experiences with other people. Perhaps longing, hoping, and expecting others to give something in return only led to disappointment. Most people have had letdowns in this way because that's the nature of the ego.

On the other hand, as you live through the spiritual heart, you don't look to someone else to fulfill you or to be the source of love in your life. Rather, you're grounded in the soul and divine presence, which contains your wholeness, love, and inner goodness. This is your inner Source of fulfillment, contentment, completion, and unconditional love.

Your heart center is a portal to your soul and divine presence. It's the place to go when you feel insecure or cut off from the presence of light or the soul. It's the place to go when anxiety, nervousness, or stress blocks access to your inner self or precludes you from feeling connected with your soul. In such cases, it helps if you explore deeply into the heart and surrender the impediment. When you accomplish this, you can discover your true home again.

Your spiritual heart is your easiest connecting point with the highest enlightened awareness of your soul. A heart center that's open to the soul is beyond beliefs, stories, concepts, ideas, and perceptions. The spiritual heart is where truth and reality are experienced and expressed because the spiritual heart holds the undistorted purity and presence of the soul.

The reason to use the specific designation *highest enlightened awareness of your soul* is that the soul is surrounded by ego layers, which can filter your connection with and your experience of the soul. When you request the highest enlightened awareness of your soul, you bypass the ego and connect with the pure, undistorted, and fully aware nature of the deep soul.

This spiritual heart is quite different from the emotional heart, which is not objective and doesn't see things as they really are. The emotional heart is greatly affected by what you want and hope, and it's also busy protecting you from the threat of getting hurt. But the spiritual heart, which is accessed deep in your chest, is the gateway to the purest and highest aspect of your truth. This is the place to come home to when you're feeling hurt, lost, or confused. When you need to call forth a power or quality, such as clarity or trust, turn to your heart and call upon the soul presence. Surrendering impediments and disturbances subsequently frees you from the karmic wheel of cause and effect.

Now let's put these ideas into practice. For the two meditations in this chapter, pick one of the four HEAL areas to focus on for healing and clearing: health, enlightenment, abundance, or love.

MEDITATION

Soul-Merge Healing

Allow yourself to settle in and get calm and relaxed. When you're ready, put your attention on whatever you sense is causing you to hold on to a reaction, block, or limitation —

whether it's related to health, enlightenment, abundance, or love.

Next, search for any beliefs you have about it. Get in touch with that first. Ask yourself: "What do I believe about this? What conclusions have I come to about this?" Summarize what you believe to be true about the situation. Take a little time to do this now.

Next, repeat in your mind:

I call to the highest enlightened awareness of my soul to merge into all these perceptions.

This engages a process, and each time you repeat the request, you go deeper into the process. Repeat in your mind:

I call to the highest enlightened awareness of my soul to merge into all these perceptions.

Now affirm:

I call upon the peace and love of all the angels and archangels to clear me and purify me of all my limitations.

This engages another process.

Notice what is in your heart space now, once you have made these requests. You begin to receive the awareness of a new presence emerging that has space for every reaction and perception that comes up. Repeat the following phrase a few times:

I call to the highest enlightened awareness of my soul to merge into all these perceptions.

Notice the responses to your requests. Sense and notice the awareness of a deepening presence that merges into your consciousness and into your issue. Hold your intention for the process while focusing on the presence in your heart. Observe what's happening in the field of your emerging presence of light and love. Just observe and receive. No thinking or doing is necessary.

While you're observing your inner space and inner reactions, you generally find inner voices attached to every perception. These voices hold beliefs, judgments, and opinions about all of your experiences. They may sound something like "I'm not good enough," "I'm not worthy," "I'm afraid," "I've been abandoned," "I'm stuck," or "I'll never be healed."

These are some of the more common voices, but thousands of others may be unique to you and your circumstances. Find and listen to your inner voices and say to yourself:

I am willing to release the need for these voices now.

Listen to your inner commentary, and surrender the need for it. Take a moment to do this now.

Healing is the process of allowing your own creations to dissolve and be replaced by a deeper truth. You unwittingly created most of what you want to let go of, and you probably don't even remember when or how you did it. As long as you're willing to let go of the pain, struggle, and conflict, you can dissolve it through surrender and embracing the enlightened awareness of your soul.

The reason the ego holds on to everything so tenaciously is that it's afraid of its own destruction and death. Consequently, it clings to anything that it thinks makes it secure or promotes its existence. But what the ego doesn't know is that the soul can take better care of you than any judgment, emotion, or position it can create. So make the commitment in your heart right now to let go of and dissolve anything you have created and carry with you that isn't leading to health, enlightenment, abundance, and love.

Your ultimate intention is a complete and total letting go of anything that causes you to fear or get upset, including any judgments or reactions. Take a gentle, deep breath now, and release anything that comes up.

After you have left this life and passed into the next, the only question you'll ask yourself is not "How much have I accumulated?" but "Did I love as much as I could love?"

Bring healing love to the parts of yourself that have been holding on to pain. Embrace the pain by calling to your own soul to merge into the darkness. Ask the soul, which is love, light, joy, and purity, to merge into the pain. Allow yourself to fill with the natural love and light that is the truth of your soul. Attune yourself to this process. You've made a request; now allow yourself to receive the gifts. When you make a request, the answer is automatic. Relief comes in the form of peace and presence.

Your request naturally brings a clearing away of the issue, which is immediately followed by a deepening state of peacefulness. This is a very deep, peaceful, calm, and expansive state that allows you to float in the embrace of divine presence. Sometimes a lightness of being accompanies it. Sometimes you might experience bliss and a sense of well-being. Everyone experiences this moment a little differently because happiness and bliss manifest in many ways. Just allow yourself to be open and receptive. Relax and rest in this receiving state for a little while.

Letting go of your past, and every thought or concept related to it, may seem like a dissolution of your identity, and this often causes the ego to pull back in fear, as if it's losing something of value. But the ego has nothing of value to lose, so what it fears never happens. The more you surrender, the more awareness emerges as you float and expand into a field of enlightenment. In fact, while the ego fears loss, you actually experience the opposite: an expansion into a greater awareness of what you really are. You'll never feel a loss except the loss of pain and struggle, so acknowledge to yourself that you feel safe to let yourself float in a wonderful and very deep and peaceful state now.

If any part of you pulls back or contracts at the idea of letting go, think of the surrender process as opening to receive what you are. This process leads only to awakening and unfolding of the most wonderful of qualities. It's about receiving the awareness of the deepest truth of your own being. Say to yourself:

I am ready to let go of all judgments.

I am ready to receive the deepest soul presence.

I am ready to open myself to receive and accept the deepest peace of my soul's core.

You're setting your intentions to receive the support of your deepest divine nature. In reality, you're only getting out of the way and allowing yourself to receive the gifts that are already there, waiting for your acceptance. You're invoking a higher presence and a higher guidance, and a response is always automatically forthcoming.

Just relax, sit back, and trust that you're receiving all

you have requested. You have invoked all the forces of creation to help you. This is the nature of creation and the heart of the soul-solution process. So simply deepen your trust in receiving.

Allow yourself a little more time to receive before continuing on.

Now, ask all you've experienced in this session to fully integrate in and through you — completely, into every fiber of your being. Express gratitude for all you've received.

Bring all of your energies and awareness into present time by saying: "I now call my body, mind, and spirit into present time, here and now." Bring yourself fully alert and aware.

ABOUT RECEIVING DEEP-SOUL HEALING

Notice in the meditation above — and in the soul-solution process in general — that we approach the clearing process in two ways, both of which are important. The first way involves identifying something that needs transforming. This is important because we usually only release what we identify; identifying and describing memories, beliefs, conclusions, and the issue or pain offer a starting place. Then we take it a step further. The second part of this clearing process is surrender, which allows you to open to, receive, and embrace a purification through merging with the light of the soul.

Refining your requests also refines the answers and responses; subtle but specific differences in your requests can lead to progressively deeper healings and realizations. This aspect of the process occurs not through analysis as much as through allowing the requests to rise into your awareness from a deeper part of you. Curiosity about important issues opens your awareness to deeper insights into what to release.

A small amount of thinking and analysis may seem to be necessary, but actually very little is required. The process requires only that you observe and recognize what's surfacing, so that you can bring the light and presence of your soul to it. Then, as you become aware of insights, you simultaneously hold an intention to let the love of the soul merge into and clear away anything that disconnects you from it. The next meditation allows you to build on this process, as you continue to let in and receive deep-soul healing.

MEDITATION

Receiving Deep-Soul Healing

Arrange yourself comfortably as you prepare to meditate. Begin by inhaling and then exhaling as if sighing — ahhhhhh. Continue to breathe in a deep, gentle manner as you send a thought and intention of love to your physical body and bless it.

Say to yourself:

I ask the full, enlightened presence of my soul to merge into me and to fill me now.

Now go deeper within yourself, and join with the love and light of the soul. Welcome the receiving and allow it to stream into and through your whole being.

The love and light of the soul merge through you progressively, going deeper and deeper, cleansing areas that you didn't even know existed, but that are now accessible to the soul through surrender. Welcome the receiving. Remember, no doing is required in this process. All depends upon receiving, so relax and receive.

Say these words to yourself:

Now, through the presence of the highest enlightened awareness and the love and light of my soul, I open to releasing and letting go.

I surrender deeper and deeper now.

The deep love is its own light and its own intelligent presence as it moves where it's needed into your issues. What you've been holding on to relaxes in this presence of deep love — a presence that allows you to let go and receive its gifts.

Ask the soul to fill your entire *belief* universe — the place where you store your perceptions and arbitrary judgments. This is a very important request, as the deep love and light of the soul can take you out of the prisons created by your mind and ego by dissolving negative beliefs.

Let yourself be cleared of all fear and anger. Let go of all resentment and hatred. Release all feelings of being hurt, betrayed, and devalued by others. Receive the deepening presence of your soul to bring light and presence to areas of darkness. Receive the clearing deeper and deeper.

Open to filling all the places yearning for the love of the soul. Let yourself receive the deep love that connects you with God and your soul. Receive it deeply inside. Receive the love deeper, and let the soul, love, and divine presence do what they do. Sit in the divine presence now, and allow yourself to receive the gifts and healing deeply into you.

Notice more peace, more beauty, more light, more love, and more presence. You might also feel lighter, cleaner, clearer, and brighter.

Receive the soul presence all through you so that your inner beauty can radiate and diffuse through the inner chambers of your being like a beautiful fragrance. Say to yourself:

I open to receive the divine radiance of the full beauty and presence of my soul.

Witness the divine, resplendent light of your soul diffusing through all the cells of your consciousness, permeating your whole being with the most sublime, precious beauty. This is truly who you deeply are.

Express gratitude for what you've been given today. Take a deep breath, and be present in your body as you smoothly and easily make a transition back to your normal, everyday activities.

Chapter 12

DEEP LOVE *and the* SOUL PROCESS

Meditating on opening the heart
to deep love melts the mind and emotions
in the ocean of love and light.

As you do the meditations in this book, you begin the process of connecting with the feelings and sensations of deep-soul love, which sets in motion the opening of your heart center. This, in turn, leads you to a deeper spiritual love.

This deep love is only accessed through the soul, and a very simple way to initiate your connection with the soul is to focus your attention in your heart and soul center in the middle of your chest and call to the soul, saying things like, "I love you, my soul," or "I feel the love of my soul."

The first few times you repeat these words, you may not notice anything different, but if you make this a meditative practice and repeat the words many times while holding a deep and sincere desire to feel the love of the soul, you'll eventually notice an extraordinary presence emerging all through you.

Your soul is you, so you can most certainly connect with it, even though you may need to practice this for a while before you're sensitive enough to feel its presence. Most people are unaccustomed to meditating in this way, and the mind distracts them from being aware of the soul's presence. By focusing on the heart and the sensations and feelings of love within the heart, you'll find that the mind and emotional reactions are left behind. Meditating on opening the heart to deep love melts the mind and emotions in the ocean of love and light.

Love is the essence of your soul. Love is more refined than the qualities of the mind; it has the ability to soothe the activities of the mind and can even replace most of its distractions. Sometimes people experience this when they "fall in love" with someone. When you take this to the next level — by entering into a deeper spiritual love — the experience is amplified further, though with spiritual love you can still access the higher qualities of the mind as the need arises.

The spiritual path of love spoken of by many great spiritual teachers requires an exploration into the mystery and depth of love. To become a lover of love in a deep way requires surrender. Although most of this process happens in a place deep within you, the mystery gradually gives way to an awakening to your divine reality.

FINDING THE DEEP LOVE OF THE SOUL

In the realm of spiritual work, your intentions bring about the reality you experience. This isn't like trying to become a great athlete, which requires tremendous discipline, hard work, and endless practice. In spiritual endeavors, you already have everything you need within, and all that you need to do is turn your attention within yourself to make the connection with your deepest soul. There, in your innermost being, in the very core of yourself, you'll find deep peace, deep stillness, and, above all, deep love. Of course, the more you do this, the more natural the experience will feel.

After you find this place of soul love, you use your intentions to become embraced by, surrounded by, and immersed in an ocean of deep, divine soul love. As you deepen into this experience, you'll find that you're in a state of deep peace and completeness. Sometimes you'll feel a warm glow resonating all around and through you. The feelings of love are much more expansive and comprehensive than analytical thoughts, so as you experience this, your thoughts will diminish and perhaps even disappear. In some cases, nothing else will remain. The mind will be empty except for the deep love. As the mind settles and quiets, it reveals an inner space where you can become more deeply aware of the presence of the love essence of your soul. The love essence is always with you, but the ego, mind, emotions, and outer distractions can seem to separate you from that presence.

THE PATH OF LOVE LEADS YOU HOME

Following the path of love returns us home because love is what we're all made from, as well as our primary reason for existence. Our core essence is constructed from a fabric of love. When you feel deep love, you're feeling your soul and spirit. So give yourself permission to feel your soul. When you imagine your own soul wrapping its arms around you and embracing you with the most comforting, warm, and loving hug, you merge into those feelings and enjoy them.

The primary feelings of the soul are peace and love, which are much more encompassing than any thought process. So as you engage the soul-merging process, and allow all thoughts and emotions to relax and disappear into the soul, you'll find yourself in the expanse of peaceful consciousness. The essence of deep love and the universal unity it reveals are the stage and backdrop to all you do. Love and unity are the essence of the air you breathe and the field on which all your experiences play out. When you're inwardly merged deeply in your soul, outwardly you see the divine reflected in all creation.

As you access the deepest secrets of love, you naturally feel and express the peace of your soul. The intelligence of deep love expresses itself through you, and it overtakes you with the sweetness of deep caring, fulfillment, completion, happiness, and joy that comes from merging with the Creator's love and the Source of all existence.

You have only to make a conscious choice to accept this love and presence into every aspect of who you are. All you have to do is surrender to the love as you sense, receive, and cultivate it within by returning to it many times throughout the day, surrendering and letting go of everything that insulates you from it.

In this chapter, I'll lead you through a heart-centered meditation that embraces the mind and emotions in the eternal ocean of love. The first stage in a heart-centered meditation is to evoke the sensations and feelings of love. You can do this in a number of ways, but the simplest way is to think of someone you love. Think of a person you love or have loved, or someone who has loved you or been kind to you. You can also envision a person who embodies divine qualities, such as a saint, angel, or spiritual being.

Start with your attention on whoever represents love to you, and allow yourself to delve into the qualities of love. Love has many different qualities. For some, the feeling of love is a warmth or a sweetness that brings a softness and tenderness, while others experience love as peace, tranquility, and serenity. For others, love brings pleasure and tears of joy. In whatever way love comes to you, immerse yourself in the feelings, merge with them, and hold all the love within your heart.

Opening into the Soul-Love Process

Ensure a space and time free of distractions, and arrange yourself comfortably for the meditation.

Take a deep breath in through your nose, and then let it gently out through your mouth. Feel your breath coming in and going out, and notice how good you feel when you're relaxed deeply inside. You have nothing else to do now, so just let go of the outer world and turn your awareness to your inner realms.

Begin to open your heart to receive love, much the way you would open your arms wide to embrace a loved one. Hold the intention to expand your capacity to feel and receive love. As you inhale, imagine you're opening to receive the peace, clarity, and love of your soul. As you breathe out, let go of whatever has been keeping you from feeling love, clarity, and peace. Invite your mind to relax and let go, and release all holding and resistance.

Focus all your intentions on opening to deep, heart-centered soul love. Let love free your mind from its activities. As you read these words, read them as though they are spoken to you from the highest enlightened awareness of your own soul.

Give yourself permission to open to receive more grace, more love, and more divine presence. Let your body and mind be pure vehicles for love. Say to yourself:

I give myself permission to receive more grace, love, and divine presence.

Surrender all resistance as you give permission for a conscious, deeper soul presence to emerge. Breathe in, and open your heart further, releasing any resistance that's keeping you from the fullness of expressing life through your soul.

Each time you go into the soul-love process, you surrender your individual consciousness into the ocean of divine consciousness and love, and the deepest divine awareness of love reveals itself to you more and more.

As the mind settles and becomes quiet, you then become more aware of the divine presence that has been waiting there for you. It's always there, of course, but the mind, the emotions, and the outer world cover it so much of the time.

Open your full receptivity to the deepest love, so that you can sense it, feel it, and embrace it. Breathe it in, and make it a part of who you are until you radiate deep love. Inhale love. Breathe love in with every breath.

This task doesn't require effort or struggle. You have the full, natural ability to receive deep love because you're made out of love. You only need a willingness to surrender and open all your receptors to the full expression of that love.

Open every cell of your body to love and soak it up. Embrace love, and let it flow in. Feel yourself dissolving into the intentions of love, and take several minutes to let yourself go and enjoy the feelings.

Through the soul-love process, you release the world of

forms and emerge into the limitless ocean of love through the deep heart. Within the deep heart, you're always one with the divine, but in order to realize this, the ego and mind have to be merged in love. The ego's world of separation is dissolved in the currents of love that are activated through the soul-love process.

Breathe love deeply in and out with each breath. Breathe love in through every pore of your body. Experience the love until you realize that love is the fullness of your nature and awareness.

As the mind becomes more still, the heart opens further, and the mind quiets further still. If you sense any pulling back, acknowledge the presence of deep love, and allow the mind to surrender and gradually become comfortable in this transition. As a wave disappears into the ocean, the mind eventually disappears into deep love.

When you initially experience this merging with soul love, it may last for only a few seconds. Just for a moment, your conscious, thinking mind disappears, but over time the mind gradually lets go for longer periods. Open a little deeper now to the expanse of the deep-love presence filling the space all around you. Welcome it in deeper and deeper. Take a few minutes to let yourself feel the love and open your heart to receive deep love effortlessly.

Follow these thoughts in your mind and connect with them:

I am willing to surrender my need for all thoughts and beliefs that I'm not worthy or capable of deep love.

I am willing to surrender and release the need to believe that I haven't practiced love long enough.

By surrendering all that you think love is, you open yourself to embrace a deeper experience of love. One of the differences between the love you've known and the deep love I'm speaking about here is that the love most people talk about is associated with an emotional feeling. You've probably used phrases such as "I feel love" or "I feel like I'm in love." The deep-soul love, however, is a love you simply are. It's not something you just feel emotionally — the kind of love that comes and goes. It's much more inclusive, expansive, experiential, and sustained.

Notice an emerging sweetness, softness, and tenderness, as well as deepened feelings of fulfillment and satisfaction, within your heart center.

Now focus on your intention and sincere desire to open your heart more fully to deep-soul love, and repeat the following statements silently, making them your own:

I surrender to deep love.

I surrender my heart to deep love.

It's my intent and my desire to be love.

I feel love.

I am love.

There are progressive levels of merging as you immerse yourself deeper and deeper into a reality beyond the mind. More and more, you feel the peace, stillness, and deep sense of well-being that come from transforming your consciousness beyond the difficulties, pain, and limitations of the mind and the senses. For a few minutes in a day or maybe longer, you'll start to sense yourself merging into a vaster reality where the problems that surrounded you much of the time in the past no longer exist. The more you practice the process of deep-soul love, the more you'll experience all of the soul's qualities.

Now, notice what you're sensing. Acknowledge and feel your heart and the soul love centered in your chest. Sense your heart center opening and expanding to embrace deep love. Placing a hand over the center of your chest often helps bring your focus there and opens your receptivity to the love.

Allow yourself to merge into the feelings throughout your body as you move deeper and deeper into them. Let the love in. Continue to notice the sensations throughout your body. Let this memory and feeling register within you.

As you activate the heart, the presence of deep-soul love slows down the mind, and the self becomes absorbed in the vast expanse of deep love. This is the beautiful journey to an enlightened state. The path to full enlightenment is through the heart, not the mind, so keep opening your heart to receive all the gifts that the open heart offers. Observe your feelings. Feel your soul and spirit. *Be* your soul and spirit.

You're becoming conscious of being a source of love. It isn't you, the person, but it is you, the essence of your soul, which is love and light. Your mind is realizing this now as you allow the soul presence to radiate through everything that you are. This is the process of awakening to your connection to the Source of all. No other comparable power-ful force exists in the universe. This is it! This is everything!

Breathe into your heart center, and imagine your heart space expanding to encompass your soul's presence as it fills you with its qualities and essence from head to toe. Let your-self relax, let go, and melt into the feelings. Breathe love into your heart and into your body. Feel the love flowing and radiating throughout your body.

As you breathe out, let the feelings of love flow from you effortlessly and naturally. Tune in to what is there, and enjoy feeling it open your heart center to receive even more love and soul presence.

Gradually allow yourself to be infused with the all-encompassing unity and presence of love that underlies all life. In the plane of unity, the true nature of all creation is an expression of oneness. In the outer world, we experience only a fragmented and separate sense of our self and our life. Here, however, everything is complete, and we come to know that everything is just as it's meant to be.

Follow these thoughts and speak them in your mind:

I open my heart now to merge more and more deeply into deep love.

I allow pure, deep love to merge deeply into my heart.

Notice what you're sensing and feeling, and merge into the feelings of the soul throughout your body as you move deeper and deeper, absorbing love. Invite deep love to fill every structure within you. Let everything within you that's unlike love melt, disappear, and vanish in the presence of love, so that only love remains.

Breathe in the purity and presence of love, accepting it into every cell of consciousness in you and around you. Feel yourself deepening into the softness, sweetness, gentleness, and richness of soul presence and love.

As you travel deeper into consciousness, you'll sense that you're dissolving into an expansive and all-encompassing ocean of love, which can sometimes seem like nothingness to the mind. But in that nothingness lives an intelligent and dynamic presence that loves and cares for you with infinite tenderness. The love that's experienced beyond the mind is total and all-encompassing. The love that belongs to the outer world is just a pale reflection of this real, deep love on the level of the soul.

The soul love is deeply complete, and over time it becomes even deeper and richer as you practice receiving it in meditation.

Now that you have been receiving and floating in the realm of the heart and love, you can extend this love, compassion, bliss, and joy to others simply with your intentions. Notice the warmth, caring, generosity, and peacefulness flowing in and through you. Let all of these feelings emanate from your heart and reach out to those who are close to you without expecting anything in return.

As you return to your normal awareness from these loving and blissful states, realize you can return to them again at any time. In fact, you can carry them with you throughout the day.

And as you put your attention back on yourself and feel loving-kindness and peacefulness permeating you, you'll discover that opening the heart brings continuing joyfulness and peacefulness.

Make the internal request now to fully integrate all you have explored in this meditation. Know and allow this integration process to continue day and night. You have engaged a process that continues indefinitely.

Express gratitude for what you've been given today, and then gently bring yourself back to normal waking consciousness.

Chapter 13

HEALING YOUR INNER CHILD

*The good news is that you can actually
reparent yourself now and give to yourself
the kind of childhood you would have liked to have.*

We turn now to look at another way we can bring the tremendous power of deep-soul love to bear on healing core issues. One of the curious things I've noticed about issues is the complex way their energy patterns and programs are stored within us. In other words, you may think you have an emotional issue, or feel that your life is stuck or that some aspect of your life doesn't really seem to work, but that's only part of the story. Components of every issue or pattern you want to release are actually stored in multiple places.

We're more complex than just a soul in a body. Our various traits are like programs running in a computer network. In this chapter, I'll be showing you how to reach deeply into that network — and all those programs — to bring deep and lasting healing.

WHAT TO CLEAR, WHERE TO CLEAR, HOW TO CLEAR

Sometimes we find that the patterns we're running are stored in more than one place in the body, and not just in the brain.

You may know this if you've ever had bodywork, such as cranial sacral work, deep massage, or some other physical modality, and during the treatment vivid memories and feelings welled up that took you back years as you relived traumatic experiences or injuries.

Actually, many of the aspects that characterize your identity seem to be programs in your body related to what you've either created or inherited. Mental and emotional patterns or programs are stored and processed in the brain, of course, but a subtle auric field around you also stores these patterns. Programs related to your core issues are also found in the subconscious mind, which often operates on autopilot, running unnoticed and keeping you on a specific course. You've probably noticed that many of your reactions seem to arise spontaneously and automatically; much of this can be attributed to the way your subconscious mind operates. In addition, the *collective unconscious* — the larger consciousness of what various groups are thinking and feeling — contains patterns that affect you on some level.

The *causal body* also exerts an influence. This "body" isn't really a body but rather is a place in consciousness where causative forces of consciousness reside. These forces bring about the circumstances of our lives. This is another way of describing karma. *Karma* is merely a word to label the forces we have set in motion in the past. Karma is composed of beliefs, conclusions, fixed opinions, and emotional reactions, and traditionally the causal body is said to hold these karmic energies. Since all people have a past, beliefs, and reactions, we all have karma. Since changing beliefs will affect karmic outcomes, your karma can change at any time.

As we've seen, in the soul-solution process, it's important to release *all* the sources and causes of an issue. If you don't, you risk not completely releasing the issue. For instance, if you release a conscious belief but you haven't cleared it from the subconscious or some of the other areas mentioned above, you may find that it recurs or that one symptom simply morphs into another. If you've encountered some challenges around releasing, clearing, or changing areas of your life, it's likely because the pattern still resides somewhere within your complex makeup.

When you're releasing an issue or pattern, it's important to hold the intention of releasing it at *all* levels. If you don't clear the issue everywhere — in all the places where it's held — you may not clear it fully. No wonder so many people seem to have been working on the same issues for ten, twenty, thirty years or more.

Thorough clearing doesn't have to be a complicated process, since most of these patterns respond to clearing techniques that entail simply holding the intention to let them go while bringing in the soul presence. That is, when you're clearing and letting go of an issue, you hold the intention of releasing the pattern from *all* the places it has been stored, while inviting the soul to merge into the pattern wherever it may be held. You can also enumerate the various specific areas that you think may be affected. Even though this is not always necessary, it's a good practice to include.

MEETING YOUR INNER CHILD

Most problematic issues begin in childhood. These patterns are found in what many refer to as the *inner child*. Your inner child is composed of stored emotions, memories, beliefs, and reactions from the perspective you had as a child. In addition, much programming seems to be stored at the cellular level or DNA level in the physical body.

Inherited factors include tendencies that have been handed down from generation to generation. What this means is that if you're from a family that has anger issues or aggressive tendencies, you may have to deal with those patterns within yourself, too. If you're from a family that has strong energies around victimization, then you're more likely to have to deal with those issues as well. These factors affect a person's deep-core conditioning.

Environmental and cultural conditioning also affects the child. A child raised in China, for example, grows up with a different set of expectations than one who grows up in France. In addition, parental and sibling influences play a key role. What children learn from their parents differs from sibling to sibling, depending on their brothers, sisters, relatives, and friends. These and other factors make up the conditioning of children, and they exert their influence from gestation in the womb through the formative years, even extending into adulthood.

Again, the inner child is composed of memories, reactions, and conclusions acquired from our childhood perspective. Childhood memories acquired in a restricted, rigid, and severe home life are retained, as are memories of a loving and supportive childhood. Knowing about the relationship of children to their family is important. If children don't feel safe at home, they may not feel safe later in life as adults. If this is the case, fear may become a prime motivator and could lead to antisocial behaviors or to feelings of self-consciousness or discomfort around other people.

Children develop a variety of behavioral compensations to deal with these patterns. For instance, perhaps they withdraw into the mind and become very intellectual, or maybe they become athletic and powerful to keep threats away. Each child compensates in a different way.

In most cultures, the relationship with the mother strongly defines the child's environment. Therefore, many inner-child issues have to do with the mother. Of course, the influence of the father is also relevant, but the relationship with the mother generally has the strongest effects. The key is to bring safety and nurturing to children by giving them a safe home and a safe relationship with their home.

Naturally, as you reflect on your own life, you may wonder what you can do about something that happened long ago. The good news is that you can actually reparent yourself *now* and give to yourself the kind of childhood you would have liked to have.

The following meditation is designed to help you explore your past and bring healing and resolution through your heart and soul center as you contact and nurture your inner child.

MEDITATION

The Inner Child's Journey Home

Make your normal preparations for meditation and arrange yourself comfortably. Relax as you reflect on the words of this meditation. Let your breathing deepen as you relax fully.

Recall yourself when you were a young child. Pay particular attention to when you were between three and six years old. In your imagination, allow yourself to feel the deep experience of meeting yourself at that age.

You may not have many memories of your life at that

time, but just imagine looking into the eyes of your own self as a child, and imagine that you're hugging your inner child. Wrap your arms around your child. Maybe your inner child hasn't been accepted this way in a very long time, if ever, so give this to yourself now. Take a minute or two to engage in this process.

While holding yourself as that young child, feel the needs the child has. Maybe the child needs love from you; maybe the child needs trust because of being left alone for a long time; or maybe the child needs to feel safe, secure, supported, and valued. Let the inner child's needs be heard as you remain relaxed. Let your inner child express whatever he or she needs to express. Take several minutes now to allow yourself to be with this exploration.

Give your child whatever he or she needs. Have the intention of beginning this giving now.

Relax and let go even deeper. Allow your inner child to receive what he or she needs and has been waiting for. Allow your inner child to be nourished by your deep love and deep caring. Let your child know you value, love, and support him or her.

Imagine, as you go further, that this is the time for your inner child to meet your soul. Imagine that your soul is standing before your inner child in its radiant light. Feel your soul breathing love and presence into your child very deeply now. You don't need to try to figure out how to do this. Your soul knows what to do. Trust that inner presence and process. Your intention is all that's needed as you allow the soul to merge its awareness into your inner child. Take a few minutes to do this.

Give your inner child permission to receive the fullness of deep healing, love, and nurturing. Allow the inner child to receive the gifts the soul has to give. Receive healing, acceptance, unconditional love, and peace.

Listen with your feelings. Let the soul and divine presence into your heart and consciousness, and embrace your child. Trust your intentions. Trust your intuition. Trust the process. Give your inner child whatever he or she wants.

Allow the presence of your soul to become alive in your body, thus reawakening your energies and connecting you with your divine essence. As you breathe in the presence of love and light from your soul, you bring it in layer by layer, deeper and deeper, into your own heart and into the heart of your inner child.

Allow your inner child to be embraced with the purity and loving arms of your soul and divine presence.

Now imagine that you are letting go of being the adult self, and you're becoming the inner child. You're becoming the little girl or boy who lives within you. Feel and let yourself be that child, fully embraced in the love of divine presence, comforted by the pure love and light essence of your soul.

Allow your soul to fill you with the light of God more and more deeply. Receive it and feel it deeper and deeper.

Let the comfort of the soul and divine presence come in more fully with every breath: Relaxing, clearing, healing, and restoring. Deeper and deeper.

Allow the love and comfort of deep-soul love to expand throughout your body, throughout your organs and tissues. Notice how this purifying light and healing presence feels.

Open your inner eyes, and look into the eyes of your divine nature. Imagine looking into the eyes of your own soul, and open your imagination and intention to receive the deep-soul healing as the highest enlightened awareness of your soul merges into all the unconscious and subconscious realms, radiating its brilliance all through you. Receive, receive, receive.

Now introduce yourself as the child within to your deepest divine self and experience who you are. Imagine yourself as the child, and take a few minutes as that little boy or girl to communicate and interact with your soul directly. Notice how it feels to receive the soul deeply into every issue your child has ever faced. Embrace every painful memory with the most healing and loving presence of your soul.

What else do you hold in your heart that you want to surrender and release to your deep soul and divine presence? Wait, listen, observe, and receive the fullness of all answers to your requests and desires. Receive reassurance. Receive support. Receive the deep love and fullness of presence, thus clearing all causes of suffering, all beliefs in lack, and all feelings of struggle. Receive the highest enlightened awareness of your soul's merging all through your consciousness, past and present. Open to receive. Receive. Receive.

Stay with your soul-merging process, and receive these

words deeply. Through the depths of the heart, feel your soul, and discover all the gifts that await you deep in your inner being.

Every level of your heart and soul contains wonderful qualities waiting to be discovered. These include the qualities of kindness, compassion, deep-healing love, eternal goodness, and deep peace. Allow yourself to feel into the rich goodness that awaits you in your soul.

Your connection with your divine self and deep-soul love is always available. Experience knowing this. Perhaps you may sense a part of you that doesn't believe it. Take in your feelings right now. Say the words you have to say at this time to surrender all concerns, so that all resistance dissolves around your unfolding. Take a few minutes to do this.

Sense how your heart feels right now. How does what you received feel in your heart? Acknowledge the healing journey of your inner child. Follow these thoughts and make them your own:

I am blessed with love, beauty, and joy.

I feel love, beauty, and joy and drink these all in, deeply.

I ask love, beauty, and joy to integrate deeply within me.

I fully integrate all of this process into the fullness of who I am in this place and this time.

I feel gratitude for all I've been given today.

Reconnect with your surroundings, and come back to your adult self now. Fully return to your present self. Take a deep breath, and acknowledge that you're fully centered and grounded in the present and fully integrated in your body.

Acknowledge and express gratitude for the healing that took place, as well as making note of anything that you'd like to work on more as you repeat this process in the future.

Gradually bring your awareness back to your normal consciousness, and continue with your day.

Chapter 14

the SOUL'S GIFT *of* ENLIGHTENMENT

It's like opening your eyes in the morning
to an experience quite different from
the dreams you had been dreaming at night.

You've now experienced the soul-solution process and deep-love healing in several meditations. As you continue the process of regular meditation to tune in to your soul and call upon its healing capacity, you'll automatically and naturally express more of your soul's qualities in your day-to-day life.

But what of enlightenment, a goal sought by so many spiritual seekers and a quality embodied by many spiritual teachers?

At the end of this chapter, I'll present a meditation designed to give you a taste of the enlightening awareness that arises naturally through surrender and grace, with your soul's help, but first let's look at what we mean by enlightenment.

ENLIGHTENMENT AS OUR
NATURAL STATE OF BEING

As I see it, enlightenment is our natural state of being. Extreme sports, the drive for excellence, scientific investigation, and, in fact, all seeking, searching, and exploration are simply humanity's ways of trying to regain the completion, oneness, and happiness of our original state.

Enlightenment is often regarded as a mysterious shift in consciousness that only seems to happen to a few. The rest of us are left to work hard to achieve it, unsure whether we'll ever get there. Yet when you discuss enlightenment with those who have gone through the experience, they tell you that they feel more like themselves than they've ever felt. They say they feel more alive, awake, and aware than ever, and they report that the process of becoming awake in consciousness feels very natural. So, what is this enlightened state that everyone wants? What's it like, and how do you get there?

Ultimately, enlightenment is about freedom at all levels of being. This includes becoming free of the judgments, perceptions, and reactions of the ego, which act like a filter between us and all of our life experiences. The mind rarely allows us to experience life the way it is. It's constantly editing and commenting on everything. Input is forever being interpreted, evaluated, analyzed, colored, and filtered by our conditioning, our past pain, and our past ideas, judgments, beliefs, conclusions, and choices. Although the mind certainly has a role to play in everyday life, it nevertheless stands as an obstacle to the freedom and liberation of the more enlightened states.

In the state of enlightenment, the mind is still present, but it functions in a different way. To give an analogy, imagine two computers, each with a different operating system. Each computer performs a similar function, but what appears on the screen and the way each machine operates are different. When you look at the computers, they look very much the same. In fact, they could be identical, but once you start using them, you find that, though they are capable of doing similar tasks, the precise way they handle these tasks is unique to their operating system. Similarly, we all have human bodies and minds, which are normally driven by the ego's operating system, but which the soul can also operate, although it does so in some significantly different ways.

The ego, as we've seen earlier, likes to be in control, and the mind is the primary tool the ego uses to run things. Because of this, some believe that the goal of enlightenment is to eliminate the mind. This is neither true nor necessary, since those who are enlightened still have minds that make it possible for them to go to the grocery store, balance their bank accounts, pay their taxes, and do the myriad other tasks that make up everyday life.

The difference is that, in the enlightened state, you transcend the way the mind operates and become free of the ego's drives and needs. This means that once you're enlightened, you can experience freedom from the need to be in control, from the tyranny of negative emotions, from the past, and from the many other defense mechanisms the ego employs to insulate itself from its insecurities and fears.

THE SOUL TO THE RESCUE

In describing the soul-solution process, I've said that it's easiest to connect with your soul in your heart center, but actually your soul fills you everywhere. Your soul is inside of you and outside of you, but it's easier to connect with your soul by putting your focus on your heart center, so that's the method I suggest. Inside the soul are many thousands of chambers or cells of consciousness holding all of your experiences, qualities, and everything else that makes up the soul. Sitting deeply inside the individual soul is an area infused with divine presence and consciousness.

When you connect with this deep aspect of the soul, you experience unity consciousness or enlightenment. This is what

I refer to with the phrase *the highest enlightened awareness of the soul*. As you integrate this state of awareness more deeply, it takes over the operation of your mind and energy field, and you no longer live your life through the drives and needs of the ego. Until this state is completely integrated through all levels of your consciousness, you may shift back and forth from the ego state to the peaceful unity state. Sometimes when this happens, people believe they've lost their enlightenment. But this isn't the case, since the soul is and has always been in a naturally enlightened state. Moving away from the soul's operating system only means that you've temporarily shifted to the ego's system, but the soul is still there, as it always is, waiting for a reconnection.

THE THREE INGREDIENTS
OF ENLIGHTENMENT

My deeper goal in all the meditations I've shared with you in this book is to take you to the doorway of enlightenment. If you're diligent with practicing the meditations, the divine Source of all will take you through that doorway. Some can do this more quickly than others, but for most it takes a number of years. For others, an entire lifetime may be required. However, regardless of how much time it takes, three ingredients can accelerate your journey to the enlightened state.

The First Ingredient: A Regular Meditation Practice

The first key ingredient to reaching enlightenment is to establish and maintain a regular meditation practice. Some sort of meditation practice is fundamental because it loosens the mind's grip and thus allows you to connect with your soul and divine presence. The more you connect with the soul at all levels through meditation, the more the soul replaces the ego's role in your life. The meditations and practices I've shared with you in this book form a good basis for your ongoing meditation practice.

The Second Ingredient: Clearing and Healing Ego Patterns

A second key ingredient to reaching the enlightened state and maintaining it is clearing or healing the ego patterns that get in the way. Engaging in transcendent meditation isn't enough unless you also remove the illusions, karma, blocks, and patterns of limitation of the ego. If you don't remove and eliminate these deeply held ego patterns, they will continue to pull you back into ego reactions and an ego-programmed life. In parts 2 and 3 of this book, I've shared with you the essence of the soul-solution and deep-love healing technique that can enlist the help of your soul in dissolving, clearing, and healing these blocks.

The Third Ingredient:
Attaining & Maintaining Positive Life Skills and Qualities

A third ingredient that's essential for reaching and maintaining an enlightened state is attaining positive life skills and qualities to help you bring forth your soul in all you do, say, and are. These skills or qualities include integrity, honesty, virtue, generosity, and self-responsibility, as well as practicing being loving in all relationships, and being kind and polite in interactions with others. By integrating these into your everyday life, you align with the intrinsic nature of the soul. Many of the meditations in this book have shown you how your own soul already has these qualities and can infuse them into you and help you anchor them in your daily life.

PUTTING THESE INGREDIENTS
INTO PRACTICE

Maturing into truly putting these three ingredients into practice is a process, and for this reason enlightenment is itself an ongoing process rather than a one-time event. This process can be compared to walking up a mountain path. As we ascend the mountain, sometimes the climb is more challenging than at other times. Walking on a spiritual path brings up whatever needs to be addressed to take us to our next level. As issues come up in our day-to-day life, we're able to deal with some easily, while others resemble the more difficult parts of that pathway up the mountain. Regardless of what they are, it's essential to heal or clear the challenges, and this is where the soul-solution process proves most helpful. When we merge the soul consciousness into every experience, the soul itself gradually becomes the predominant presence in our lives.

Remember, you are pure consciousness expressing itself through a body, a mind, and an individualized soul. As you integrate your soul into your everyday experience, you come to see that the soul has its own intelligence and knows exactly what you need, when you need it, and how to bring it to you in the best way. The soul-solution process can facilitate many of the classical states of enlightenment — such as causeless and unconditional love, deep peace, limitless joy, oneness, ecstasy, and bliss — because these are all inherent qualities of the soul.

Awakening to enlightenment includes not only moments of insight but also sustained experiences of absolute happiness; a witness state or sense of being a neutral observer of all that's happening around you; oneness with God or Source and the entire universe; a connection to all people, animals, and things; a sense of understanding everything about life; an automatic awareness of being in the present moment; feeling in love with life; a deep, unconditional love for everyone; a natural compassion and caring for all creation; an absence of emotional charge regarding past events, people, and traumas; an internal state unaltered by external conditions; and a quiet and peaceful mind.

All of these elements and more are already natural qualities of your own soul. The soul-solution process frees your life-force energy to help you achieve your greatest dreams. It frees you from the drama of an ego-dominated past as you step forward to truly enjoy your life.

Enlightenment is also sometimes called *self-realization* because you realize who and what the self is, and this provides entry into a state of internal peace, love, and completion that totally eclipses what you thought you might have been seeking through power, control, possessions, other people, recognition, obsessions, or other strategies of the ego. You awaken to the truth of yourself and discover that you have all the fulfillment and happiness that you've been seeking.

Again, enlightenment is a developmental process, not a one-time event, although significant awakening experiences can happen along the way. Looking at the universe and all the life in it, we see that everything is in a process of becoming. Nothing is static. The latest insights from quantum physics indicate that an infinite number of universes exist in constant creation and evolution, and that we're all aspects of that intelligent creation. *Enlightenment* is just a word for the process we're all already undergoing. We don't need to confine it to a narrow definition because it represents the unfolding of our potential in all aspects of body, mind, and spirit.

THE ROLE OF GRACE

Grace plays a key role in surrender and enlightenment; indeed, nothing of true value can be revealed without grace. *Grace* is one of those words frequently associated with religion, but it has a meaning far beyond what most people think.

Grace is a type of gift because it's something you receive, but not from any other person or even from yourself. It's a gift that only comes from the Creator, the Source of all. No other source could supply it, and it's the most precious gift there is because it awakens your awareness to the truth of your being, which is something that underlies all perceptions and judgments. Grace leads you to discover your inner being and your true self, and ultimately it allows you to achieve self-realization and to awaken to the enlightened state of consciousness.

Grace is sometimes described as an "unmerited favor" from God, and it certainly is that, since there's nothing you can pay for, bargain for, work for, or strive for to get enlightenment. Any of these would be equivalent to the ego's trying to enlighten itself, which is impossible. On the other hand, we've already discussed three ingredients that can help you arrive at the place where you're ripe to receive the gift of enlightenment: having a regular meditation practice, clearing and healing ego patterns, and attaining positive life skills and qualities. The final ingredient underlying all three is the mysterious gift of grace. In order to become enlightened, which means to release the ego's needs and drives, we need something beyond the ego to come into play. And the grace of our divine Source is definitely something far beyond the ego.

Grace is traditionally described as a gift from God for development, improvement, and character growth. It's necessary because it enables people to overcome limitations that would otherwise be insurmountable. In the sense that limitations are all ego characteristics, this is true. Grace or enlightened awareness is necessary for us to transcend the perceptions of the ego and its limitations. But in another sense, this isn't exactly true, since all the limitations the ego perceives are really illusions generated by perceptions and interpretations. None of these limitations are actually real or true, but perceiving them to be true makes them true to the perceiver. This is where grace comes in because grace is about transcending illusions.

Grace comes when we truly surrender. By letting go of all judgments and all resistance, we release the ego's attachment to control and discover that we don't need it. Grace is completely letting go of the past in every form, at every level, and in every way. When you truly surrender, something beyond your conscious awareness takes over, and you remain open to receiving the gift of liberation from illusions while awakening to the truth of your being.

Receiving the gifts of grace requires surrendering and letting go of all ego projections, including fear, shame, guilt, anger, hatred, resentment, unworthiness, arrogance, guilt, judgment, criticism, blame, and other ego identities. Once you've surrendered all of these things, liberation opens before you automatically, by grace, carrying you into an awareness of, and an awakening to, truth.

Remember, you can't earn grace, you can't control grace, and you don't have to deserve it. You just have to surrender limiting ideas, beliefs, and feelings, and realize who and what you are. Then you naturally return to your real home in unity.

THE POWER OF GRATITUDE

One way of practicing surrender and opening to grace, in addition to those we've already talked about, is to practice gratitude.

When you say thank you for both happy and challenging experiences, your act of gratitude will open doors. Gratitude relaxes and releases resistance, enabling you to be available to receive.

You can practice gratitude by saying: "I am thankful for all the people in my life. I am thankful for all the plants and animals on Earth. I am thankful for art and music. I am thankful for all memories and dreams. I am thankful for all the goodness in my life." You can expand this practice to include all you see and experience in your life, including your challenges.

This may sound simple enough, but gratitude actually includes a little more. For example, often instead of being happy and content with what you have, you may find that the ego greedily wants something more, better, or different. Of course, the ego can't be grateful while it's making comparisons or wanting and desiring more. So being grateful at all times for all things requires practice. Once again, surrendering what the ego wants opens you to what the soul is, which allows gratitude to flow naturally and automatically.

Grace operates outside of the typical human ways of doing things. People want to believe they're in control. In fact, people feel like they need to be in control in order not to feel out of control. As a result of this natural ego component, people assume they can do specific things to ensure they are rewarded. Since it seems to the ego as though most things in life are earned through hard work and effort, people expect that work is also required to "rise to the top" spiritually. People expect the "gifts of God" to be given out according to some recognizable plan that entails rules, conditions, prerequisites, and effort. To some degree, we certainly have a role to play: We need to show up, be available, participate, surrender, and let go of whatever we've been holding on to. But ultimately grace is freely given, not earned in any way.

EFFORTLESS EFFORT

Another aspect of receiving grace is to be open to *effortless effort*. Most people go through life working at what they do, seemingly fighting through a daily grind, while others seem to move forward with amazing ease. *Effortless effort* is a state in which the world seems to be working *for* you rather than you working for the world. It's a state in which your life has an ease and flow, undisturbed by surrounding storms, because you're in the peaceful eye of any storm. Even hard work doesn't feel oppressive, burdensome, or laborious.

Effortless effort isn't the same as inertia, laziness, or passivity. Rather, it's a state of nonresistance. It feels like swimming with the current and going with the natural flow of life. When you allow the divine presence to work through you, all your actions take on a natural flow that has an effortless quality. As a result, you flow with all of life's experiences and feelings as they come and go.

Effortless effort sounds a bit like nondoing, which is a very difficult idea for most of us to absorb because we're so used to doing, doing, and even more doing. Effortless effort, however, isn't at all the contradiction it sounds like. Existence itself requires obvious effort. You get up in the morning, get yourself ready, eat, and do what lies before you for that day. All of this takes effort, but the energy behind the effort has an ease and flow to it because you have surrendered to the process and are not in resistance to anything. Therefore, you're automatically in a state of harmony and synchronicity.

When you're not engaged in thinking, doing, forcing, pulling, pushing, demanding, struggling, straining, wanting, or needing, the ripples of the mind naturally subside, and a deep peace, quiet, and stillness open before you. In these moments of total surrender, completion comes to you. Without any effort, by grace, you enter an expanded field and float in the ocean of consciousness.

THE FINAL RELEASE

Now we turn to a most important subject: the final ego release and the dawning of enlightenment. Grace applies to all the steps leading up to this culmination, but the last and most important one is the final release. This is when all resistance in every form lets go, which is only achieved through deep, complete, and total surrender. All ideas, beliefs, fears, perceptions, reactions, and desires are released.

At this point, something truly incredible happens. The idea of letting go to this degree may create thoughts that everything will be lost, but what happens is the opposite — the complete dissolution of separation with a concomitant awareness of being one with all. At this level only one awareness exists — the one we call God, the Tao, or Source. It's the absolute, undifferentiated awareness that underlies all existence.

This experience is indescribable. To even say there's a sensation and a realization isn't quite accurate because it's truly beyond words. As soon as words are used to define the experience, it falls short. That's why it has been said that the truth shall never be written, not because it's something to keep secret, but because words can't express it. It's a state in which everything is understood, everything is fulfilled, and everything is complete. And this all happens through grace. While you do what's necessary to arrive at the threshold through surrender, you then automatically and naturally awaken through grace. It's like opening your eyes in the morning to an experience quite different from the dreams you had been dreaming at night.

Grace is the awakening or enlightening of your awareness to the truth of your being that underlies all your perceptions and judgments. Surrender leads you to the place where you can receive the grace that awakens you to the enlightened state of your inner being, to your true self, and to God realization.

In the following meditation, I'll guide you through a process to give you a sense of the gifts surrender and grace can offer.

MEDITATION

Opening to Surrender and Grace

Arrange yourself comfortably for this process. Take a deep breath in through your nose. Hold it for just a moment, and then let it slowly out through your mouth and feel yourself relax.

There's nothing else that you need to do or even think about at this time. Acknowledge that this meditation is the most important activity for you to do in your life right now. Therefore, you're totally free to release and dissolve any tension or concerns and open yourself to discover transformational insights.

Let the body be soft and open. Let the awareness be gentle and allowing. Now turn to the inner-soul presence in your heart center. Follow these words now and make them your own:

I ask my soul and divine presence to emerge in my heart and my body.

Allow awareness in. Sense and feel softening. Let space begin to open all around your heart area. Say to yourself:

I feel my soul deeply in my heart.

Gradually open more and more.

I feel my soul deeply in my heart.

Dissolve all else but the purity of divine awareness. Receive the moment-to-moment deepening of soul presence in an open and soft heart space.

Explore your inner space as you continue inviting in soul presence. Sense it coming in. Repeat:

I feel my soul deeply in my heart.

Open to receiving. Open to divine grace and acceptance. Allow and receive openness, spaciousness, and grace. Explore any sensations that arise, and soften into the peaceful presence of your soul.

I feel my soul deeply in my heart.

Receive a deepening sense of peaceful presence. Acknowledge a purity of the soul's soft, healing light.

Feel merciful compassion for the part of you that has experienced struggle and suffering. Hold a comforting, nurturing, loving, and healing presence for those memories, feelings, and thoughts of pain and suffering. Imagine you're embracing yourself as if you were embracing your only child. This helps merge the soul presence into the pain and relieve the suffering. Meet everything with an allowing soul awareness.

Have mercy on the voices of pain, and bless them with an invitation of divine grace. Listen as they all melt away.

Say these words to yourself again, and hold the intention of deepening into the feelings:

I feel my soul deeply in my heart.

Enjoy a sense of floating in soft, open awareness, and receive the presence of your soul as you merge deeper and deeper into its presence. Surrender and receive grace, healing, and freedom. Let go and release all of your perceptions, and float in the vast ocean of grace and acceptance.

Receive grace and the fullness of your pure soul bringing your highest divine presence into your awareness. Your path home is a path of surrendering all the positions your mind creates in order to embrace the highest awareness of your soul's presence fully.

Surrender involves a willingness to release and let go of your way of seeing things to accept the higher soul's view. This always leads to receiving mercy, love, acceptance, and the grace necessary to take you to your next revelation of awareness. Moving to the next step in your spiritual evolution involves nothing more than this process.

Let the highest enlightened awareness of your very soul flow into and merge into you. Invite your soul to merge into all your judgments and thoughts. Receive the clearing, release, and healing of all of your issues. Allow yourself to feel all of this.

This is the place where you allow yourself to dissolve in love and the soul presence. Meet all sensations with forgiveness, compassion, and healing awareness. Melt into infinite gentleness and kindness toward yourself and toward all you have suffered with over lifetimes. Allow yourself to receive grace and love in infinite, unconditional acceptance and caring.

You have made some requests, and the nature of reality is that you always receive responses. Let your heart melt into the deep acceptance, humility, and willingness to receive the inner presence of the highest enlightened awareness of your soul to guide your being and be your healing.

Be with your heart space, and give yourself permission for it to expand its opening to receive even more of your highest soul presence as the eternal gift of grace and love.

You may have sensations of something shifting or changing. As you deepen your surrender and your trust, you may sense a lightening in your body and in the space around you. You may notice a lightness of being.

Notice any differences in what you perceive around you. Allow yourself to receive the answer to your requests.

Say to yourself:

I invite the enlightened presence of my deepest core truth to merge fully and completely into my mind and being.

Notice whatever you're experiencing in response to your requests. What do you sense?

The way to bring enlightened presence and soul awareness through you is by requesting it and surrendering. This subsequently opens you to grace. Say these words:

I deepen into divine presence and awareness.

I open my heart to receive the healing presence of grace to fill me completely.

I receive the healing presence of grace deeply, without conditions.

I open my heart to receive the purest divine presence into my heart.

Allow yourself to be cleared and transformed. Feel yourself being cleared deeper and deeper. Sense yourself receiving, clearing, and experiencing the lightness of the soul's presence.

Slowly attune to the inflow of divine peace, love, and light merging throughout your being and erasing all causes of all issues.

Now say yes to accepting what you're receiving, and be aware that when you say yes, you become aligned with your soul and with divine presence. You are the love and light of God. You are one with God, with Source.

Feel into the receiving and deepening of surrender to what grace is bringing to you. Let the higher light and the true self that you are come in deeply. When you do this, you realize unity with all.

Repeat these words to yourself:

I ask the highest enlightened soul presence to merge into my mind and all my beliefs.

I ask the highest enlightened soul presence to merge into my past all the way back to the moment of my creation.

I ask all of these requests to fully integrate in and through all levels of my consciousness, completely and deeply into every fiber of my being.

Notice the presence of peace. Notice the subtle changes within you and within your being. Become attentive to the awareness and sensations that are present with you. Notice the peacefulness. Notice the sense of well-being. Recognize that these gifts come to you through grace. Receive the blessings deeply into you.

Inhale the blessings all the way through you, and let them stream into your heart and body. Receive all the gifts of grace through divine presence. Say these words to yourself:

I integrate the core of my enlightened nature through all levels of my consciousness.

As peacefulness fills you and the light moves within you, surrender to the beauty and love opening all around you. Carry the pure vibration of the soul's love and light. Say these words to yourself and integrate them deeply:

I feel love, beauty, and joy.

I feel gratitude for all I've been given today.

Slowly allow yourself to come back to your normal state of consciousness. Maintain your connection with the deep place within you. Now take a deep breath, and be fully present in your body. Come back and be totally awake and aware. Know that you are blessed with love, abundance, and grace as you live through the highest enlightened awareness of the soul.

Conclusion

the LIGHT of the SOUL

The soul light within you seeks
to connect you with the greater light in everything,
much the way a river is determined to merge with the ocean.

As you engage with the meditations in this book and allow yourself to experience your soul's love and light, you begin the process of surrendering your mind and opening your heart to your soul. As you do, an inner light emerges and radiates through your whole being.

Many paintings depict saints and holy people with radiant light around them and familiar halos above their heads. This is the light of the soul. Such images show how deeply the surrendered individual's entire inner being becomes luminous from head to toe with the light and presence of the soul.

Of course, the light of the soul isn't a physical light that everyone can see, although many are able to naturally tune in to subtle energies and perceive a radiant light around people. Some who've engaged in meditation practices can actually see the light of the soul, appearing as a brilliant white light. Some call this inner light the *ultimate light*, the *absolute light*, the *light of consciousness*, or the *light of creation*. Here I'll simply call it the *light of the soul*.

As we engage with life and the five senses take over, our awareness of subtle energies, including the light of our soul, diminishes. Our intuitive senses become submerged under layer upon layer of energy patterns composed of emotions, judgments, needs, doubts, successes, and failures. The inner light is still there, of course, but we don't notice it. As we engage in spiritual practices, such as reading inspiring books, singing spiritual songs, reciting mantras, and meditating, we can at times feel illuminated. As the light and presence of the soul emerges, it reveals a feeling of inner presence.

At such moments, we sense something beyond the range of the five senses — our connection with the divine consciousness within all life. Often such experiences are only short glimpses as the distractions of our regular life once again take over. But even short experiences of the inner light intimate that our life extends beyond the senses to engage a much larger universe. Awareness of this larger realm subsequently fuels our search to connect further with the light of our underlying nature.

An amazing characteristic of the inner soul light is that it emerges simply when we put our attention on it. In other words, the more you engage in activities that put you in touch with your soul, the more you feel its inspiration and presence. By connecting with the light of consciousness, you can sense and feel the light and soul presence emerging and embracing you. In fact, all creation is composed of intelligent and loving light, and the more you connect with it, the more you feel its presence and experience its many gifts. Our home is truly in the light, and light contains the qualities of our true nature.

Imagine what your life would be like if everything you thought, said, and did were guided by your pure and enlightened soul. Imagine if all of your daily choices and decisions arose from your soul. Your life would be wonderful in so many ways. For instance, the negative ego would disappear, and there would be only one voice within you — the loving voice of your soul and divine nature. You would be full of deep love every moment, and you would be happy and fulfilled because you would have surrendered all blocks and resistance.

All of these outcomes happen when you spend time every day connecting with your soul in meditation, continually deepening your surrender to the light of your soul. The light is in us, through us, and around us all the time. Qualities such as love, peace, joyfulness, and beauty abide within you and within us all. When your heart is pure and your focus is on your inner presence of light, these inherent qualities awaken automatically.

I can think of no more fitting conclusion to this book than to offer you a meditation to guide you once again into the light and the realm of your soul. I hope you will return to this experience again and again, and allow your own soul to be your guiding light all the days of your life.

MEDITATION

Basking in Soul Light

Assume a comfortable, meditative position, and breathe easy, gentle breaths. Imagine that you're breathing in golden white light through the top of your head. Bring this light down through your body, and let it radiate out through every pore.

Open yourself to receive more and more replenishing and rejuvenating life-force energy with each breath. As you bring in the light, sense it clearing your mind and your body. Keep relaxing as you settle into a peaceful state.

Set aside anything you were thinking about earlier, and be present with this process now. Acknowledge that this meditation is the most important thing for you to be doing right now.

Give your body permission to release any tension or resistance it is holding.

With each breath, feel yourself floating and expanding as the light grows all around you. Feel peacefulness and light integrating into all the cells of your body. While this is occurring, say to yourself:

I ask my soul to emerge in my heart and rise to the surface.

I invite the divine light of my soul to surround me and fill me.

I feel receptive to inviting the light of my soul to fill me.

I give myself permission to merge completely into the pure light of my soul.

I allow myself to receive more and more light.

I feel and allow the light of my soul to permeate deeply into me.

I allow the light of my soul to radiate through my cells, tissues, and organs.

I love the light, and I feel the light.

I feel suspended in an ocean of divine love and light.

I merge into the light, and the light engulfs me.

With each breath, fill the cells of your body with more light. Fill the organs and systems of your body with light.

Open your heart to receive the soul's light, and let it radiate all through you. Be relaxed and open and receive the light without conditions.

Open your heart very deeply, letting love and light radiate from you. Allow the presence of the soul and light to dissolve all the places of suffering, struggle, and pain. Surrender everything to the pure, white healing light of the soul.

I embrace the light.

I feel embraced by the light.

The light of my soul is love.

I live in the light, and the light lives in me.

The light of my soul willingly releases and dissolves all resistance.

I ask the light of the highest enlightened awareness of my soul to integrate all through me.

Light is already within you, so request that the light merge fully into you. Imagine you're floating in an ocean of comforting light.

Feel relaxed in your soul's light. Acknowledge the light, and let it embrace you.

The light that is everywhere is the loving and intelligent light of creation, and it's also the light of your soul.

You can keep repeating your affirmations, and more and more radiant light will fill you each time you ask. Say these words to yourself:

I allow divine love and light to expand through me.

I give myself permission to merge completely into love and light.

Deepen into the acceptance of the love and light that fill you. This acceptance is your truth. This is who you are. This is also your destiny. Love and light are always present and alive within you. Observe that a part of you is aware of meditating and sensing the connection with your divine presence. Say to yourself:

I ask for more and more pure light of love.

I accept the pure light of God into every atom and cell of my being.

I feel the light of my soul expanding and radiating from my heart.

Acknowledge and sense the essence of love and light moving and expanding from you now and radiating from your heart like a blazing sun of love energy.

You are a source of radiant love. Hold everyone in your life in the embrace of love and light. Ask to integrate the love and light of the soul into your everyday life. This love and light is who you are and will continue to flow through you naturally and automatically.

You are always and continually an openhearted, radiant source of deep love and light to everyone and everything around you.

Feel and express deep gratitude for everything you have received in this meditation.

Return in your own way and in your own time to your full, normal everyday consciousness. Reconnect with your body and surroundings. Let the light of your soul shine forth throughout the rest of your day.

May you be blessed with love, abundance, and grace, and may you always live life through the highest enlightened awareness of your soul.

ABOUT *the* AUTHOR

For over thirty years, Jonathan Parker has been a counselor, author, and creator of one of the largest libraries of audio recordings for personal enrichment and self-directed growth in the world. His unique, spiritually based methods go far beyond traditional motivational and self-help techniques, empowering others to rise to an enlightened life and develop their innate potential.

His wide spectrum of programs tap the deepest reservoir of human capabilities and inspire success in achieving the highest of human potentials. His programs have touched the lives of many thousands, lifting them to achieve personal excellence and financial success, vibrant health, winning performances, and the heights of the human spirit.

His recordings, workshops, and retreats offer inspiring and life-changing experiences. *The Soul Solution* is his first full-length book in a planned multibook series to be published over the coming years. Jonathan lives with his wife, Jackie, in Ojai, California. Audio programs of meditations similar to those in this book are available at www.jonathanparker.org.

H J Kramer and New World Library are dedicated to publishing books and other media that inspire and challenge us to improve the quality of our lives and the world.

We are socially and environmentally aware and strive to embody the ideals presented in our publications. We recognize that we have an ethical responsibility to our customers, our staff members, and our planet.

Our products are available
in bookstores everywhere.
For our catalog, please contact:

H J Kramer/New World Library
14 Pamaron Way
Novato, California 94949

Phone: 415-884-2100 or 800-972-6657
Catalog requests: Ext. 50
Orders: Ext. 52
Fax: 415-884-2199
Email: escort@newworldlibrary.com

To subscribe to our electronic newsletter, visit
www.newworldlibrary.com